OUR FAITH

BY

EMIL BRUNNER

TRANSLATED BY JOHN W. RILLING

CHARLES SCRIBNER'S SONS · NEW YORK

1954

To My Sons

Printed in the United States of America

C-6.56[MH]

This book, now for the first time translated into English, was published by Gotthelf-Verlag, Bern, under the title *Unser Glaube*.

FOREWORD

"Man shall not live by bread alone, but by every Word that proceedeth out of the mouth of God." That is no simile, but a literal law of life. There is a pernicious anæmia of the *soul,* a starvation of the *soul* as well as of the body. Humanity in our time suffers from chronic under-nourishment of its soul. It is not sufficient help merely to print and sell copies of the Bible; not sufficient help, even, if men read it. The Bible can nourish us only if it is understood and personally appropriated as God's own Word. But for many—whatever the cause may be—the Bible is indigestible; it does not speak to their need. Such people seek, therefore, an interpreter to translate the great, difficult, strange words of the Bible into the familiar language of daily life. The performance of this task, in my opinion, is the true service of theology,—to think through the message of God's work in Jesus Christ—think it through so long and so thoroughly that it can be spoken simply and intelligibly to every man in the language of his time.

In a time like ours when all outward securities are shaken as perhaps never before, many are beginning to listen to Truth which is not from man. A new hunger for the Word of God is passing through the world—the English-speaking world no less than Europe and the East. The Word of God is the one thing which is able to unite East and West, the whole dismembered mankind, and to reshape it into one big family of nations. It is a special satisfaction to me that this little book after having been translated into several continental languages,* can now appear simultaneously in both English and Japanese. May it help in bringing to our consciousness that we are all called to one aim as we are all created by one Creator after His image.

EMIL BRUNNER

Zurich, August, 1936.

**Our Faith* has appeared in French, Dutch, Danish, and Hungarian translations; a Czech edition is in preparation (*Translator*).

CONTENTS

CONTENTS

OUR FAITH

1. IS THERE A GOD?

The only answer to such a question is that of the Greek philosopher, who, when asked about God by an idler, kept a persistent silence. To the merely inquisitive question, "Is there a God? I should be interested to know whether or not there is one," silence is the sole possible answer. Or perhaps one should reply to such a questioner: No, "there is" no God! "There is" a Himalaya range, "there is" a planet Uranus, "there is" an element radium: in short there are a multitude of things about which the encyclopædia gives information. But "there is" no God. That means, for the inquisitive there is no God. God is neither an object of scientific investigation nor something that we can insert in the treasure of our knowledge, as one mounts a rare stamp in a special place in an album—there it is, finest and costliest of all.

God is not something in the world, the eternal being, the divine inhabitant of the world. God is not in the world at all, the world is rather in God. God is not within your knowledge, your knowledge is in God. If your question were answered, "Yes, there is a God," you would depart with one more illusion, for you would then suppose that God is in a class with other objects.

That, precisely, is what God is not—if He is really God. God is never in a class, never something among other things. He can never be named along with other things. Planets, mountains, elements are objects of knowledge. God is not an object of knowledge. It is only because of God that anything is to be known at all. Without God there would be absolutely nothing at all, without God a man could know nothing. Knowledge is possible only because God is. The question about God is a possibility only because God already stands behind the question. If you really enquire about God, not with mere curiosity, not, as it were, like a spiritual stamp-collector, but as an anxious seeker, distressed in heart, anguished by the possibility that God might not exist and hence all life be vanity and one great madness—if you ask in such a mood as the man who asks the doctor, "Tell me, will my wife live or will she die?"—if you ask thus about God, then you know already that God exists; the anguished question bears witness that you know. Without knowing God you could not so ask about Him. You want God because without Him life is nonsense. Your own heart distinguishes between sense and nonsense; it knows that sense is right. Your heart knows something of God already; and it is that very knowledge which gives your question existence and power. You wish that there might be a God, for otherwise everything is ultimately the same—evil is not evil, good is not good. You know already that there is a God, for you know that good cannot possibly be the same as evil. The observation of the evil in the world, and anxious questionings about it cause you to doubt God's existence; but the very fact that one sees and questions is belief in God. Because your heart knows God it protests against wrong. In the act of asking about God, God is already standing behind you and makes your question possible.

Not only the heart within, but the world without also testifies of God. I have never known chance to create order, so that the meaningful and beautiful arise out of mere chance. To believe that the world is a creation of God is not credulity. Credulous, rather, is the belief that the human eye, or the structure of an insect, or the glory of a spring meadow is a product of chance. The rock cairn which the wanderer sees on a mountain peak —not chance, but a hand has laid these rocks one upon the other. Yet a million times more beautiful than such a stone heap is the retina of the eye. It is truly no evidence of intelligence to miss anything so obvious.

It is really a sign of mental disorder when a man asks, "Is there a God?" One might almost say that this is the question of an insane man,—a man who can no longer see things simply, clearly and calmly as they are.

Something of this madness however, pervades the whole world, and we all feel its consequences; one might indeed call it the distinctive madness that afflicts our modern life. Men have always asked—as far as history gives us information—"In what way shall we think of God?" but never before, "Is there a God?" Technical and scientific success has gone to our heads and confused our senses. We discard as mere chance all that we cannot bring under the mastery of our reason. We suppose that we alone create order and art in the world—missing the obvious suspicion that to make something ingenious we must first have an ingeniously created brain and ingeniously created hands. What we do create is but the creation of brain and hands which we very certainly did not create!

To ask the question, then, "Is there a God" is to fail to be morally serious. For when one is morally serious he knows that good is not evil, that right and wrong are two different things, that one should seek the right and eschew the wrong. There is a divine order to which one must bow whether one likes to do so or not. Moral seriousness is respect to the voice of conscience. If there is no God, conscience is but a complex of residual habits and means nothing. If there is no God then it is absurd to trouble oneself about right—or wrong. It all comes to the same ultimate chaos. Scoundrel and saint are only phantoms of the imagination. The man who can stop here must probably be left to go his own way.

Still—if God really does exist, why then must we always be asking about Him? Our heart cannot escape from God; it knows about God! But our heart does not know Him truly. Our conscience tells us *that* God is, but does not know *who* He is. Our reason testifies of God and yet does not know who He is. The world with a million fingers points toward God, but it cannot reveal Him to us.

Who is God? What does He want of us? What purpose does He have for the world? To these questions *we* know no answer—and so long as these questions are unanswered we do not know God. There is another, and only one other, possibility: if God chose to reveal Himself *to* us we could know Him truly. *That* God exists is testified by reason, conscience, and nature with its wonders. But *who* God is—God Himself must tell us in His Revelation.

2. IS THE BIBLE THE WORD OF GOD?

No one will dispute the assertion that the Bible is a unique Book. It is noteworthy, if for no other reason, in that so many people possess this Book and so few people read it. Why does every one have a Bible? Why is this Book translated into so many hundreds of languages? Why is this venerable Book reprinted again and again in millions of copies annually? Two hundred years ago, scoffing Voltaire, probably the most famous man of his time prophesied that all would soon be over with the Bible. The house in which this boast was made is today one of the offices of a great Bible society. Voltaire's name is almost forgotten; the Bible has had, in the meantime, an incredible career of triumph throughout the world. What is it about the Bible? Whence these facts?

The immediate answer is quite plain: because the Christian Church believes the Bible to be the Word of God,—just as the Mohammedan is persuaded that the *Koran,* and the Hindu that the *Bhagavadgita* is the Word of God; and because Christians are the most proficient propagandists, the Bible is the most widely disseminated Book. Quite right. But this is to overlook one thing: the Bible not only comes from the Christians; Christians come from the Bible. One might make the statement: there are Bibles because there are Christians. Primarily the reverse is true: there are Christians because of the Bible. The Bible is the soil from which all Christian faith grows. For if there were no Bible we should know nothing of Jesus Christ, after whom we are called Christians. Christian faith is faith in Christ, and Christ meets us and speaks to us in the Bible. Christian faith is Bible faith. What is meant by that statement?

Who is God? What is His purpose for us? What are His plans for the world, for humanity, for you? You cannot know that of yourself; nor can any one tell you that. For what you yourself cannot apprehend of God no one else can know either. After all, he is only another man and no man can answer these questions of his own accord. God alone can do it. But *does* He? Does He tell us? Does He reveal the secret of His world plan? Does He make known His purposes for you and me and for all mankind? Christianity answers these questions with an emphatic Yes, God has made known the secret of His will through the Prophets and Apostles in the Holy Scriptures. He permitted them to say who He is. And what they all say in different words is fundamentally the same thing, just as seven sons of a good mother speaks each in his own way of her. Each one says the same thing; and yet each says something different. So, too, the prophets all speak of the one God, not only as eternally enthroned above all temporal change, the invisible spirit above all earthly affairs, but as the One who has purposes for man, who does not leave man to his own devices like some great nobleman who says: I can get along without them; I can wait until they come to me. Not so God. He who alone is the great Lord, does not act as does the nobleman who proudly holds that the poor serf must come to him. God has mercy on men; He even comes to those who do not come to Him; He troubles himself about them, follows after them like a good shepherd after his erring sheep. For He wants to gather them, to bring them home; He does not want them to remain lost; He wants them with Himself.

That is God's purpose. He therefore calls His people, now coaxing, now threatening, now from the heights, now from the depths. But He not only calls; He himself comes to them. In their error, the Good Shepherd seeks His lost sheep, gives even His life for them. It is of this Good Shepherd God that the Bible speaks. The voices of the Prophets are the single voice of God, calling. Jesus Christ is God Himself coming.

In him, "the Word became flesh." That means, in him *is* present that which these Prophets and Apostles were not, but of which they could only speak. They can only *speak* of the Good Shepherd. Jesus himself *is* the Good Shepherd. The Prophets and Apostles can only point like doorkeepers to the coming one and say: see him yonder, there is he whom we await. They can open the door: now he stands there, himself! He *is* the Word of God. In him, his life and death, God proclaims His purpose, His plan, His feelings. "I have revealed to them thy name." He is the Word of God in the Bible. Is the whole Bible God's Word then? Yes, insofar as it speaks of that which is "here" in Christ.

Is everything true that is to be found in the Bible? Let me draw a somewhat modern analogy by way of answering this question. Every one has seen the trade slogan "His Master's Voice." If you buy a phonograph record you are told that you will hear the Master Caruso. Is that true? Of course! But really his voice? Certainly! And yet—there are some noises made by the machine which are not the Master's voice, but the scratching of the steel needle upon the hard disk. But do not become impatient with the hard disk! For only by means of the record can you hear "the master's voice." So, too, is it with the Bible. It makes the real Master's voice audible,—really his voice, his words, what he wants to say. But there are incidental noises accompanying, just because God speaks His Word through the voice of man. Paul, Peter, Isaiah, and Moses are such men. But through them God speaks His Word. God has also come into the world as man, really God, but really *man* too. Therefore the Bible is all His voice, notwithstanding all the disturbing things, which, being human are unavoidable. Only a fool listens to the incidental noises when he might listen to the sound of his Master's voice! The importance of the Bible is that God speaks to us through it.

How then, are we to regard those other books which claim to be God's word also? There are two things to be said: first, are you a Mohammedan or a Hindu? If not, then these books do not apply to you. Second, if you still want to know how we are to regard those other books, I can tell you only one thing: a different voice is to be heard in them than that which we hear in the Bible. It is not the same God, not the Good Shepherd who comes to His sheep. It is the voice of a stranger. It may be that somehow it is God's voice, too. But if so, a scarcely recognizable voice, just as a poor photograph may resemble you, but not at all look as you are.

Now are there any other questions? It is my opinion that if this is the way the matter stands, there is only one conclusion to be drawn: Go now, and begin at last to listen attentively to the Master's voice.

3. THE MYSTERY OF GOD

Any one who speaks of God as though He were a cousin, about whom, naturally, one knows everything, really knows nothing at all of God. The first and most important fact that we can know about God is ever this: *we* know nothing of Him, except what He Himself has revealed to us. God's revelation of Himself always occurs in such a way as to manifest more deeply His inaccessibility to our thought and imagination. All that we can know is the world. God is not the world. Therefore He is also exalted above all our knowledge. He is Mystery. Not simply a riddle, for riddles can eventually be solved,—some sooner, some later. That God is mystery means that *we* cannot solve the enigma. "Can'st thou by searching find out God?" To man's proud "not yet" the Bible replies "not ever." Such majesty is like a profound abyss, whoever looks into it becomes dizzy. "From everlasting to everlasting"—who can understand that? He who was in the beginning when there was as yet nothing, and through whose will all things that are have arisen—who can ever conceive of such a thing? To think of the mystery of God makes us feel vain and petty, we remember that we are dust.

There is, however, another thought that abases us even more; that God is the Holy One. Probably every one remembers from childhood what impression it made upon him when he was told, "God's eye sees you continually. He even sees into your heart, and there is nothing in you that God does not know." For we knew quite well even then that this *seeing* is also *judging*. God is not simply a spectator, God is the Lord. That means God wants something. He wants what he wants without condition. There are men of great will power about whom one perceives that they know what they want. Mysterious influence, something of almost crushing power radiates from such men. But what is human will power! No man wants anything absolutely, thereunto even the strongest will is much too weak. Even an iron will can be bent, deflected, paralyzed. For every man there are conditions under which he simply will not go on, but God's will is absolute. He wants to be absolutely Lord of all. If He did not want that, He would not be God. But that He does will, that He wants unconditional obedience to Himself, this thought really humbles us utterly. "The holy God" destroys us even more than "the almighty God." When the Prophet Isaiah heard the song of the cherubim, "Holy, Holy, Holy is the Lord," he answered, "Woe is me for I am undone." The holiness of God is like a powerful electric current, whoever touches it dies.

What if we refuse to do what God wants, what He absolutely desires? When we will not obey Him, what? Imagine an automobile driven by a madman. He will not permit a wall to block his way. "I won't stand for that," he says, and opens the throttle wide and rushes against the wall. That is a simile for the man who is disobedient to God. He must simply dash himself to pieces aganst God's holiness. God's holiness is absolute. The disobedience of man shatters upon God, God resists the proud—is more trustworthy even than the natural law of gravity. It is just this unconditional trustworthiness of God which is the salvation of the world. For without it everything would fall into disorder. God's righteousness stands like the mountains. He who withstands God must shatter himself upon God. This is the meaning of God's wrath. Because God's will is absolute obedience He therefore hates disobedience absolutely. He who persists in disobedience falls under the fearful wrath of God. That is the holy God.

But the mystery of God is even greater. The will of this holy God—what He absolutely desires, is love. His feeling toward us is infinite love. He wants to give Himself to us, to draw and bind us to Him. Fellowship is the one thing He wants absolutely. God created the world in order to share Himself, He created us for fellowship, and that He might have fellowship with us. For that reason, too, He did not permit the world and the humanity which did not want Him to follow its own devices, but hastened after it as a mother follows her faithless child into all the byways of the city until she finds it. Though every one showers discouraging advice "be ashamed for running after the ugly thing, he never really deserved it," the mother can say only, "I am still his mother." So, too, is God. It is this which He has shown Himself to be in Jesus Christ. It is not too much for Him to descend into the lowest depths of human filth, to be bespattered and befouled as He pursues His child that it may not be lost. "For the Son of Man is come to seek and to save that which is lost." That is the God of mercy.

We must keep this endless and merciful pursuit in focus with what we said of the majesty and the holiness of God in order to understand the greatness of His love. There is nothing remarkable in a beggar lending a hand to a beggar. But whoever heard of a king dismounting from his horse to take a beggar's hand? That the heavenly King, whose majesty is inconceivable, comes down to seek His unfaithful child in all his squalor, is the love of God as the gospel and only the gospel knows. And we, the beggars, should know what sort of King it is who has come down to us. We should be terrified by the Holiness of God and our sin, that God may then make our heart obedient through His love. God desires one thing absolutely: that we should know the greatness and seriousness of his will-to-love, and permit ourselves to be led by it. Our heart is like a fortress which God wants to capture. He wants to capture it with His love. If, overcome by His love we open the gate, it is well with our souls. If, however, we obstinately close our hearts to His love, His absolute will —then woe to us! If we refuse to surrender to the love of God, we must feel the absoluteness of His will as wrath.

4. CREATION AND THE CREATOR

The first word of the Bible is the word about the Creator and creation. But that is not simply the first word with which one begins in order to pass on to greater, more important matters. It is the primeval word, the fundamental word supporting everything else. Take it away and everything collapses. Indeed if one rightly understands that which the Bible means by the Creator, he has rightly understood the whole Bible. Everything else is involved in this one word. But if! Do men know the Creator? Do they know what it means to say, God thou art my Creator?

It is not because of God that we do not know Him thus. For just as in a royal palace everything is royally administered, or as in a great artist's house the whole house testifies of the artist, even if he is not seen, so, too, the world is the house of the Great King and the Great Artist. He does not permit himself to be seen; for man cannot see God, only the world. But this world is His creation, and whether conscious of it or not, it speaks of Him who made it. Yet in spite of this testimony man does not know Him, or at least not rightly.

Every man has two hands each of which is a greater work of art than anything else that human ingenuity has created; but men are so obsessed with their own doings that they acclaim every human creation and make a great display over it, yet fail to discern God's miraculous deeds. Every one has two eyes. Have you ever thought of how astounding a miracle is a seeing eye, the window of the soul? Yes, even more than a window; one might even call the eye the soul itself gazing and visible. Who has so made it that the hundred millions of rod and cone cells which together make sight possible, are so co-ordinated that they can give sight? Chance? What harebrained superstition! Truly, you do not behold man alone through the eye, but the

Creator as well. Yet we fools do not perceive Him. We behave ourselves in this God-created world (if one may use the clumsy simile) like dogs in a great art gallery. We see the pictures and yet fail to see them, for if we saw them rightly we would see the Creator too. Our madness, haughtiness, irreverence—in short, our sin, is the reason for our failure to see the Creator in His creation.

And yet He speaks so loudly that we cannot fail to hear His voice. For this reason the peoples of all ages, even when they have not known the Creator, have had some presentiments of Him. There is no religion in which there is not some sort of surmise of the Creator. But men have never known Him rightly. The book of Nature does not suffice to reveal the Creator aright to such unintelligent and obdurate pupils as ourselves.

The Creator has therefore given us another, even more clearly written book in which to know Him—the Bible. In it He has also drawn His own portrait so that we must all perceive that He is truly the Creator. The name of this picture is Jesus Christ. In him we know the Creator for the first as He really is. For in him we know God's purpose for His creation.

God first revealed Himself to the children of Israel as

the Creator. At that time the world was replete with religions, but they did not honor the one Lord of all the world. The gods of the heathen are partly constructions of human fantasy, partly surmise of the true God, a wild combination of both. The great thinkers like Plato and Aristotle spoke indeed of a divinity that pervaded all things. But they did not know the living God. It pleased God to reveal Himself to the little people of Israel as the Lord God. That means—the God whom we may not use as one uses a porter—as the heathen use their gods. And as the God whom one cannot conceive as the philosophers think of Him, an "idea of God." But to Israel He was revealed as one who encounters man and claims Him as Lord. "I am the Lord thy God." "I will be your God and ye shall be my people." The Lord is He, to whom one belongs wholly, body and soul. The Lord is He who has an absolute claim to us, because we, and all that in us is, come from Him. The Lord God is also the Creator God, and only when we know Him as the Lord God do we know Him rightly as the Creator. The heathen, even their greatest thinkers, do not rightly know the difference between God and world, between God and man, between God and nature. These are all confused with one another. God first revealed Himself to Israel as the One who is over all the world, as its *Lord,* of whom, through whom and to whom it is created. That a divine being created the world—is not faith in the Creator, but a theory of the origin of the world, which signifies nothing. That God is the Creator means: *thy* Creator is the Lord of the world, *thy* Lord, you belong to Him totally. Without Him you are nothing, and in His hand is your life. He wants you for Himself: I am the Lord thy God, thou shalt have no other Gods (idols) before Me. That is as much to say: thou shalt love the Lord thy God with all thy heart and with all thy soul and with all thy strength. That is no lovely, interesting theory about the origin of the world; if you believe this, you are a "slave of God," your life then has another meaning, then you are really another man. Rather, you are now for the first time a man. To believe in God the Creator means to obey God the Lord.

5. GOD'S PLAN FOR THE WORLD

Looking down at night from the mountain top upon Zurich, the traveller sees a broad luminous strip in the midst of the confusing welter of the twinkling lights of the city. It is lovely and attractive although one does not understand the significance of this aggregation of lights. It is the park square in front of the railway station; each one of the hundreds of lights is in its place, but the wayfarer on the heights above knows nothing of this perfect order. Only the chief electrician knows why this arrangement has been made and not some other. He has the blue-print and can grasp the whole plan at a glance; it is his insight, his will that orders and guides the whole.

Just so, too, we may think of what takes place in the whole world. We poor insignificant humans are set down in the midst of the whole wild world and cannot survey it all. Here and there it may be, we can catch a glimpse of the wonderful order in nature, the regularity of the stars, scattered over the wide spaces of the universe yet obedient to one law; the order to be found even in the microscopic world, as also within visible things concerning which science has given such amazing information in recent years; the order in the construction of a flower or of an animal, from the flea to the whale, a noteworthy obedience to law even in the life of man. When, however, we ask, what does all this mean, what is its purpose, we know nothing definite.

We can advance clever theories and make guesses,

and men have been doing so for ages and have expressed most curious opinions about the purpose of the happenings in the world: Each one has made his guess from the center of his tiny circle of experience. But who would want to build upon such a foundation? Who would dare say; yes, it is thus and so? Every one realizes that these are only humble opinions concerning something too sublime for our conception. We know neither where we nor the world are heading. In spite of all experiment and experience it remains for us a profound, impenetrable mystery. And that weighs heavily upon us. It is as though we were feeling our way in the dark. Whither? Why? What is the meaning of everything? What is the goal? Because we do not know that, we are apprehensive, despondent, troubled, like a man condemned to hard labor without knowing the reason why. Because we have no insight into the plan of the world we are dull and apathetic.

There is One who knows the destiny of the world, He, who first made the sketch, He who created and rules the world according to this plan. What is confusion for us is order for Him, what we call chance is designed by Him, thought out from eternity and executed with omnipotence. It is indeed much to know

"He thrones in might and doeth all things well." Chance? With this sorry word we merely admit that *we* do not know why things happen as they do. But God knows; God wills it. There is no chance, no more than any light in the station below just happens to be where it is. The chief Designer knows why, while we say, "chance," "fate." It is important to know that.

Indeed, in His great goodness, God has done even more. He did not want to leave us in the dark, for it is not His will that we should go plodding through life fearful, troubled, and apathetic, but that we, mere men though we are, should know something of His great world plans. He has, therefore, revealed to us the counsels of His will in His Word. He has not done it all at once—men would not have understood it at all. But, long ago, like a wise teacher He laid his plans. To Abraham, Moses, and the prophets He revealed more and more of His plans, making them ever clearer, until at last, "when the time was accomplished" He revealed His heart and let men behold what He had in mind, His goal. Then He brought forth His plan out of the darkness of mystery and revealed it to all the world: Jesus Christ, the Word of God in person, God's revelation of the meaning of universal history so that we need no longer walk in darkness but in the light. How different God's plans are than the ruminations of man upon the riddle of the world! We spell out this great Word of God—Jesus Christ—reconciliation, salvation, forgiveness of sins, promise of eternal life, fulfilment of all things in God's own life. That is God's plan for the world.

Perhaps some one expresses himself, "It's all right with me if it comes out that way." Unfortunately that is not the way things happen in God's household. To be sure, it is only by the grace of God, through His free gift that we can have a part in His kingdom. But the man who says, "It's all right with me," has no part in it. God's help is something that comes by grace, not something that comes "of itself" like the change in voice which comes naturally at the age of puberty. God refuses to deal with us on these terms, for He wants our heart. He does not hurl his grace at us, like a bricklayer throwing mortar at a wall. God calls us to salvation. He invites us into His kingdom, he wants us to hear His summons, believe and obey Him. For it is only through such obedience that one understands anything at all of God's world plan; only he who hears the call receives light, he alone "walks no more in darkness" but in the light of God. He alone knows, through God, the destiny of all things, or rather where God will bring all things. To hear this call, and in this call to hear where God will lead us, to have insight into God's plan for the world—that is faith.

6. GOD AND THE DEMONIC ELEMENT IN THE WORLD

"And were the world with devils filled, all waiting to devour us. . . ." Who can deny that this is a bedevilled world—the world in which we live? One glance at the newspaper suffices to establish this fact. Accidents, crimes, catastrophes, famines, epidemics, revolution, war and preparations for war. "And you dare to claim that this world is God's creation? ruled by a God who is love? Are you deranged?" What reply shall we make? I would propose that we answer frankly, yes, we are deranged. That is one thing the Bible tells us about ourselves, and hence, too, about our world. Can you imagine God's creation of the world as a sort of book set in type by the printer; everything is in the right place and makes good sense when one reads it; and then while the typesetter is gone, a scoundrel confuses the type. Everything is "de-ranged," whole sentences are inverted, others are utterly meaningless. Will you accuse the typesetter of setting up a madman's book?

It is so with our world. God's "composition" has become deranged through evil, sin. As it is written in the parable, an enemy came and sowed tares among the wheat. There is something opposed to God and to the creation in this world. The Bible speaks of a power inimical to God, a leader of all diabolical powers. But it speaks still more of the ungodly power which we all know only too well out of our own experience, concerning which we know quite well that it is opposed to God. This opposition is sin, which means rebellion against God's self-will, our own stubborn resistance to God's "composition." As surely as God is love, is my own lovelessness ungodly, diabolical, resistance against God's action. Whenever an unkindness is done, God's will is not done. Rather that occurs which God does not will.

So then God does not really rule in this world? When a father merely observes, for a while, the petulant, headstrong actions of his little son so that the lad may experience for himself where his own will leads—does that mean that the father is a weak parent, who cannot control his son? He will, no doubt, take things in hand at the proper moment, but he prefers not to lecture his son, but rather to educate him through experience to make his own decisions. There is no doubt that God could, if He so desired, create order in this topsy-turvy world all at once; He could, no doubt, make us obedient with a wave of His hand. But He doesn't want to force us; it is His desire that we should turn to Him of our own free will. Hence He gives us, situated as we are in this deranged world, His Word, namely, the Law and the Promises, that we perceiving the insane folly of evil and the fixed nature of His love, may return to Him in freedom and gladness. For this reason He has given Himself in Christ Jesus to this deranged world, permitting the world to rage against Him—the madness of men, the crucifixion of His son, He has made the revelation of His ineffable love. It is there He shows us how He is master of this perverse world—so much master, that He can even employ its madness to reveal His love. God there produced His masterpiece, if we may express it so humanly, by showing that He is Lord even of the greatest darkness in this world, that men even in rebellion against Him still remain tools in His hand to be used as He wills.

If we were compelled to discover God simply by

means of the world as it now is, the thought would probably occur to us that there are two kinds of Gods, good and evil, redemptive and destructive. But in the cross of Jesus Christ we perceive that destruction is not God's will, and that in spite of it God keeps His masterly grip upon the world, and accomplishes His counsels of love. He gives us time to decide for ourselves, to turn to Him. And He gives us signs enough of His steadfast creative loyalty in the midst of this deranged, bedevilled world, that we may be able to find our way. "Yes, but how are we to explain all the evil, the wrong and the suffering from the love of God?" Dear friend, who has given you the task of explaining all this? A man who proposes to "explain" God's government of the world is even more ludicrous than the raw recruit who wants to explain the general's plan or a shophand who criticises the organization and management of a mammoth industrial enterprise. Man, what do you understand of the government of the world! "Thou art not the regent, creation well to guide" the hymn rightly phrases it. It is enough for us to know that God Who rules in a manner inconceivable to us in this deranged world yet rules by means of the Cross of His son. Let us give heed to the signals where God gives them, that we may understand His will. God transmits His will to us in the darkness of this world. It is to be found in the commandments and the gospel of forgiveness and salvation. To that we must cleave, foregoing the desire to decipher out of the darkness His will for ourselves. The solution of the world riddle will not come until the day of salvation.

7. ETERNAL ELECTION

Our life is "superficial" without depth or meaning so long as it does not have its roots in eternity. Either it has eternal significance or it has no significance at all. Temporal sense is nonsense. The Bible permits us to see this eternal depth: "thine eyes did see my substance yet being unperfect, and in thy book all my members were written, which in continuance were fashioned, when as yet there was none of them." We do not just happen to exist. Although we were begotten and born of our parents, we come from eternity, from the eternal thought and will of God. Before anything comes into existence it has been thought and willed by God, as the work of art is in the mind of the master before it is put on canvas or paper, or in stone. Deep, deep are the roots of our life. Far beyond all temporal visibility it roots in the divine invisibility, in the eternal "counsels."

It was something profound when this God-rooted quality of life was revealed to the author of the 139th Psalm. But we feel even the Psalmist had intimations given of a destiny as deep as his revealed origin. That God's eye saw us in eternity, signifies not only an eternal origin; it signifies an eternal destiny.

When God "beholds" a man, it is written, He looks upon him graciously. His face is against the man with whom He is angry. When a man is permitted to perceive that God sees him from eternity, when the eternally beholding eyes of God rest upon him and his view meets God's eternal vision, the greatest thing that can happen on earth transpires. A man then knows that God loves him *from* eternity and *for* eternity. God has chosen me from eternity to eternity. That is the faith, the full, whole evangelical faith—election from eternity. Such a man knows that he is saved without his effort, out of this evil world and age, out of the depravity of sin and death. It is God's grace alone. His mercy, His boundless love, His election alone is the basis of my salvation. That is a Christian's greatest joy. When the disciples returned to Jesus from their first independent missionary journey and enthusiastically reported how much they had been able to do by God's power, the Lord replied: Rejoice not that the spirits are subject to you, rejoice rather that your names are written in heaven! When a man knows that his name is written in the Book of Life, in the Book of Election, he knows whence comes the peace that passes all understanding. He has then climbed the highest mountain of faith, and there remains then in this life nothing higher than the preservation and the operation of this greatest, most glorious discernment.

This discernment, however, is not given to any one for the purpose of constructing theories or speculations on how it now stands with others. You are elected, and with you every one is elected who believes; every one is elected who has truthfully spoken the "yes" of decision for Christ. The elect *in themselves* are only "them that believe." And believers are those who in their hearts "have become obedient to the Word of God." Election dawns upon no one except in the full, independent, obedient and trustworthy decision of faith. It is to those, who have served the Lord by serving the least of this world, that the Lord speaks in the last Judgment "come ye blessed of my Father, inherit the Kingdom prepared for you from the foundation of the world" (Matt. 25:34). Election and obedience, election and personal decision of faith belong inseparably together in the Bible. One cannot play election off against decision, nor personal decision against election, tempting though that be to reason. Reason must bow here, yet dare not abdicate. How the two can be reconciled, the free eternal election of God and the responsible decision of man is a problem we cannot understand. But every believer knows they are compatible. "He came to his own—and his own received him not; but as many as *received* him, *to them* gave he power to become the sons of God, even to them that believe on his name." Without faith Christ means nothing to us; without Christ there is no faith. Which is more important—light or vision? Stupid question! Vision and light belong together. Therefore, believe, and you will perceive that you are elected.

This is the message of the Scripture. But of double predestination—that God has chosen one from eternity for eternal life and has rejected the other from eternity to eternal damnation, there is no word to be found in the Holy Scripture. One can scarcely avoid drawing this conclusion from the teachings of the Scripture. Logic always misleads in that direction. But the Scripture itself does not do it, nor should we. We should leave the Scripture as it is, unsystematic, in all its parts; otherwise we pervert its message. The Scripture teaches a divine predestination of election; it also teaches the judgment of the unbelieving. It teaches, too, that nothing happens without God's will, but it never teaches—let me repeat it—even in one single word—a divine predestination of rejection. This fearful teaching is opposed to the Scripture, while the doctrine of eternal election is not only according to the Scripture, but truly the center of the Holy Scripture, the heart of the Gospel; reason cannot fathom this. That is always reason's fate with the Word of God. The dogma of Double Predestination is a product of human logic which cannot withstand the a-logical teaching of the Scripture. Let us rejoice in our eternal election, let us be wary of defection! Let us say with Paul: "We who are saved," and let us be warned of him: "He that standeth let him take heed lest he fall," for he cannot then escape the Judgment. The life of the Christian, like a door hung upon two hinges, must swing upon this promise—and this warning. If it slips out of the one or the other it ceases to swing true.

8. THE MYSTERY OF MAN

What is man? No other question is so important as this one. As war or peace may depend upon the stroke of a pen in the hands of a single government official, so your life depends upon the answer to this question. The man who believes in his heart that man is an animal, will live like an animal. In a certain sense and within certain limits the statement is true, you are what you believe yourself to be. What is man? One can give various answers to this question which are not untrue. One can, for example, say that man is a chemical mixture of lime, phosphorus, and nitrogen. The Bible says it more simply—man is dust. That is true, but there are other judgments. One can say, man is a machine, or rather a factory with an enormous number of complicated machines, the stomach for example, a combustion machine. This is not untrue either, but it is not everything that can be said. One can say that man is an animal, and who would contest the many similarities which we have in common! We shall probably have to leave the question of our corporal relationship with the animals to the natural scientists. They are quite possibly right.

Yet men have always somehow known that man is more than animal, and it is verily a peculiar kind of scientific method which can no longer see the differences that separate man and beast and machine. The animal possesses understanding, no doubt, but has no reason. It has, no doubt, the beginning of a civilization, but no culture. It probably has curiosity and knows many things, but it has no science, it probably plays, but it has no art. It knows herds, but not fellowship. It probably fears punishment, but has no conscience. It probably realizes the superiority of man, but it knows nothing of the Lord of the World. Man is something other than animal, as the animal is something other than a plant. But what then is he—man? If he is no animal, perhaps he is a God. That sounds absurd, yet this madness is quite prevalent among us today. Fundamentally, say many, man and God are identical. Human reason is the same as divine reason. The soul is identical with God. Indeed this insane idea is very seductive when one rightly ponders it. For is not "God in us?" That man "fundamentally" is God, has been stated not only by ancient heathen, but also by many modern thinkers, even by many of our German idealistic philosophers. In spite of all that—it still is false. Man is not God because he is God's creature. He is not divine "in his deepest nature" because in his deepest nature he is a sinner. How is it possible that two such mutually exclusive concepts of man could be championed from ancient until modern times—man, an animal; man, a God? The Bible gives us the answer to this question, for it tells us what man really is.

The Bible first tells us, God *created* man; man, like the worm, like the sand of the sea, like the sun and moon, is God's creation. That means that man *is* what he is because God has so made him. He has received his life, his existence, his peculiar being from God, precisely as the thousands of animals have their characteristics from God. Whether or not God has employed an evolution of millions of years for the purpose of creating man is the critical concern of the natural scientist; it is not a critical question for faith. When I say God created man, I do not therewith deny that man originates from earthly parents. God uses human parents to create men. Man in the first place, then, is a member of this earthly world which comes and goes, changes and grows. Man is dust of dust. But like the dust, gloriously created of God, even more marvellously than plants and animals.

In the second place the Bible says that God created man *in his own image.* It is only of man that this statement is made. That he is created in the image of God distinguishes him from all the other creatures and makes him somehow similar to God. For what is it that is expressed by the word "image" but similarity of some sort? As a further cause of this similarity the Bible states "God breathed into him the breath of life and he became a living soul." What distinguishes man from the rest of creation is the share he has in God's thought, that is, reason as distinguished from mere perception, which the animal also possesses. Man can think into the eternal and infinite.

We must now make a third statement, God created all creatures by His Word. But He created man not only *by* His Word, but *for* and *in* His Word. That means, God created man in such a way that he can receive God's Word. *That* is reason in its true sense. Man really becomes man when he perceives something of God. We are men when we perceive the divine Word. If a man, for example, had no conscience he would not be man but in-human. Conscience is in some way the perception of the voice of God. Man has been so created by God that he can become man only by perceiving God, by receiving God's Word and—like a soldier repeating a command—repeating God's Word. God says, I am thy God. True man should say, Yea, Thou art my God. God says, Thou art mine. True man should say, Yea, I am Thine. When he says that in his heart *homo sapiens* becomes *humanus.* Previously he has been inhuman. God created us in His image, as reflections of his image. That means we are human in the degree we permit God to speak to us. We are man to the extent that we let God's Word echo in our hearts. We *are* not simply men as a fox is a fox. But we are men only when God's Word finds an echo in us. To the degree that this fails to happen we are inhuman. No fox behaves unnaturally because a fox comes finished from the hand of God. It is created *by* the Word, not *in* the Word. But man is created *in* the Word, which means that man can say yes or no to that for which God has created him, to that which God has destined as the goal of His creation. Then man becomes either human or in-human. The freedom to say yes or no to God is the mystery of man. We have this freedom from God because He has addressed us. Were God to cease speaking to us, we could answer no more, either yes or no. We would then have ceased to be men. It is in this way God desires to have an image. Men who love Him who first loved them, who reply to Him who first addressed them, in free acknowledgement, in faith. The mystery of man is the mvstery of faith!

9. ON THE GOODNESS OF MAN

Is man good? Whoever reads this question will wonder how such a question is possible, for men are different. There are good and bad, there are very bad and less bad, very good and less good men. Experience proves the truth of this observation again and again. There are quite selfish men who ask for nothing but their own profit, shysters in business, tyrants in the house, men with an interest only in what is to their advantage. And there are others who give themselves freely, often making astounding sacrifices, thinking ever and only of others, desiring nothing but to serve others and to do good. A person who fails to see this difference is blind to reality. Between the two extremes of good and evil there are as many variations in men as there are between the red and the blue of a rainbow. One can indeed say that there is no wholly bad man—each has somewhere some good in him—like that atrocious Chinese bandit leader, who relentlessly slaughtered thousands, but nevertheless played heartily with children as though he were himself an innocent child. And one is also compelled to say, there is no one wholly good—there is a flaw in each person of which one must say, there he fails. But most people are in between, a little more inclined to good, or a little more inclined to evil, according to their natures.

This view of the matter is quite correct, it is indeed necessary. But the Bible speaks differently. "There is none that doeth good, no, not one." "For all have sinned." In that passage Paul does not imply that even the best have somewhere some little evil flaw. On the other hand, "all" means that fundamentally all are in the same condition, namely bad. For "a sinner" does not signify that there is something bad in him, as a splendid apple may have a little bad speck that can be removed with a twist of the paring knife, so that you can scarcely see that anything has been cut out. No, by a sinner the Bible means "bad at heart," infected with evil at the core. "All are sinners" does not mean then that even the best are not quite saints. It means rather that the difference between so-called good and so-called bad no longer comes into consideration.

How is this view to be reconciled with what we first characterized as correct? That is not hard to say. We have spoken of what holds true among men, and there it *is* true so far as human affairs go. But before God the matter is otherwise. It is not as though God did not see the distinction between good and evil. How should He, who sees all things, fail to see that! It is not at all immaterial to Him whether a pupil takes pains with his writing, or whether he scribbles. How then could it be a matter of indifference to Him whether one belongs to the good sort or the bad? That it is a matter of concern to God, the Bible proclaims loudly enough. But on that level and within that sphere where Paul writes "all have sinned" these "good and bad" considerations have really no significance. Let me clarify this assertion by an analogy.

Two men board a train. One of them perhaps does something sensible, the other something stupid upon entering the coach. But as they look out, both notice that they have taken the wrong train and are going in the wrong direction. That one man was reasonable and the other stupid is a difference between these two men; it is a difference, however, which has no significance in relation to the fact that *both,* whatever their individual differences, are going in the wrong direction! This is what the Bible means by the word *sin,* the total perverse direction of our life, the tendency away from God. In this train all men are travelling, says the Apostle. He himself, one of the most blameless, according to human opinion almost a saint, says of himself quite clearly, "O wretched man that I am, the evil which I would not, that I do; the good that I would, I do not."

To simplify matters, let us speak of you and me, instead of all men. So far as I am concerned I find that what the Apostle says of himself applies absolutely to me too. How is it with you? Would you like to contradict the Apostle and say, "My dear man, I don't understand you, you have disappointed me. I at least am no wretched man who wants to do good and does evil instead." Can you say that—not before men, but before God?

Sin is a depravity which has laid hold on us all. It is a radical perversion from God, disloyalty to the Creator who has given us so much and remains so loyal, an insulting alienation from Him, in which all of us, without exception, have shared. I emphasize the "shared." For is it not true that we are all connected with one another by hidden roots, like the runners of a strawberry patch, all of whose plants have developed from the one parent stock? We are not only connected with each other in our life-root but our connection is precisely evil. There is a kind of common "sin fluid" that flows through the whole root system, and yet each individual knows it to be his own guilt. Explain this guilt as I will—as inheritance, bad education, etc.—it is finally my own fault. I know that I am involved in the evil of others, and at the same time I implicate them in my own evil. As far back as I can remember, I recall that I have had a bad conscience before God. And still I know, just when I think of God—it is my guilt. One cannot explain this, evil, sin, is forever inexplicable. What one can explain is not really evil; for what we explain we make ourselves superior to, we become master of.

Am I then in sin? Is this really so? How do we know for certain? Not every one knows it. Most people know only what we first mentioned, that there are good and bad people, and of course they count themselves for the most part among the good or even the better class. But what we said about sin we do not apprehend for ourselves. We do not perceive it until God casts His light like a dazzling beam into our dismal gloom.

We know what sin truly is because and since Jesus Christ died for man's sin. It is as though a great boulder lay across the road. That isn't so big, one thinks, and tries to push it to one side of the road, but it won't budge, it is too heavy. Then a strong man comes along; it is too heavy even for him. And then a horse is brought and even the horse drags it away only with the greatest effort. We measure the weight of the boulder by the effort and power required to remove it. So, too, is it with sin. It is not until we see how much it cost God to remove the stone between us and Him, that we understand how great was the weight of sin's guilt. Christ shows us how completely the whole movement of life is in the wrong direction. It is primarily he, in whom God addresses us the most earnestly, who shows us our condition. Not until then do we lose the courage to say that man is good. Then, and then only are we ready to hear the message of forgiveness and salvation.

10. THE LAW

Every Swiss knows what a law is, but no man, I fear, has as much trouble in understanding what the Bible calls "law" as the Swiss. In Switzerland the law is something that the citizen himself has made. For "the people is sovereign," which means, the people is its own lawgiver. But in the Bible law means not what comes *from* man but what is given *to* man. To understand this, let us think first of all of the so-called laws of nature. That a suspended object will fall to the floor when the string is cut is a law of nature; even the free Swiss burgher can do nothing about that. It *is* so because God has made it so. The earth takes 365 days to complete its course about the sun, this is a fact which not even a national election can establish or abolish. It *is* so because God has made it so. Or, take the laws of thought. That 2 and 2=4 cannot be altered even by a world school congress or the unanimous agreement of nations. It *is* so because God has made it so. Every man must submit to it. Every one knows that too—even the most inveterate Swiss Democrat. Here is compulsion, there is no choice about it.

But are there laws of God only where there is no choice to be made? Many think so today. Man is free, he can do what he wants. Who will have the temerity to interrupt him? You know the tale of "The Fisherman and His Wife" as told by Grimm. It is the story of modern man. Man has discovered that he can do all things, he can convert a waterfall into electric power, and make the finest pigments out of coal; he has shaken off the Lords of the Middle Ages and become "sovereign." He pierces mountains, binds seas together, alters the face of the earth; he can do all things, nothing daunts him. He is his own Lord, whom shall he permit to interfere? He can even be his own God.

Can he indeed? He can of course try it, according to the story of Adam and Eve in Paradise, and the end is ever the same. Evil comes of it. Man always overreaches himself. He can have a strong voice, but when he essays to drown out the thunder, his voice cracks, becomes ludicrous and ugly; and he may even lose it on account of the strain. So it is, too, when man tries to play God. Great as man is, he is not the Creator, and that will be evident one day when he is shut up between six boards and lowered into a hole in the earth, not so large as the tiniest hall closet. There he lies and decays, the would-be Lord God. Yes—*then* there is no choice about *that!*

No, man cannot do what he wants. For he belongs to Him who created him. As great as man is, he does not possess this greatness in his own right. It is all borrowed, bestowed greatness, it is a "gift," and a condition is attached to the gift. The more man is given, the more is expected of him. By whom? By the one who has given the gift, as is to be read in the Parable of the Talents (Matt. 25). Man is no proprietor, but a tenant; therefore a reckoning will be demanded (cf. the Parable of the Vineyard, Matt. 21). And the accounting will be demanded on the basis of what he should have done with his gifts according to the will of God. The will of God is the law. The law is what God desires of us.

Every man, Jew or Christian, believer or atheist, cultured or uncultured, has some knowledge of this law. Every man has the consciousness of "responsibility"; every one observes that he cannot do what pleases him or seems profitable, that there is a "thou shalt," and a "thou shalt not." And even if he claims to be ignorant of such things, his conscience gives him the lie, his conscience that accuses him when he does what he ought not, or does not do what he ought. There has never been a man without a conscience. The law of God is as though it had been engraved in the human heart.

But God found it necessary to reveal his law in an especial way. While lightning and thunder flashed and rolled upon the peak of Mount Sinai, Moses received the Law, and gave it on tables of stone to the people of Israel. Something of the dread of the holy majesty of God the Lawgiver trembles in the narrative of this event (Ex. 19:20-32), and rightly so. That is something to strike terror into our hearts when God the Creator, the Almighty, the Righteous, and Holy says to us, "Thus and thus shalt thou do, and thus and thus shalt thou not do." Not because He requires something should we fear. For He desires nothing but what subserves life; God's law is not arbitrary. In His law God tells us nothing but the natural laws of true human life, you must do so and so if you want to live a human life; as the physician says, you must live so and so if you wish to remain healthy. This counsel is nothing fearful, but God says, *I* desire that you should so live, human not inhuman, creatively not contrary to nature, and this *"I desire"* is what terrifies us. For when God says, "I desire it," we know what is at stake. God is in earnest, He is not mocked; whatsoever a man sows, that shall he also reap.

God requires an accounting, He holds us responsible. And that is what strikes terror in us, for how can we bribe the judge in this case? Or thinkest thou that God will wink at evil? That is the (I must add it) cursed frivolity of our generation, that it thinks God does not take things seriously, He will not cast off any one because of disobedience. Forgiveness has been misunderstood to mean indulgence. But the opposite stands in the Holy Scriptures. God will cast off the disobedient, for what men sow they must also reap. God is *Holy,* which means, He takes the Law seriously. God's law is as inviolable as the laws of nature. God is not an indulgent father, who cannot punish—just as little as He is a moody or passionate father, who punishes in a fit of anger. God is a *just* God who repays according to deserts. And is not that cause for terror, dear friend—that God holds you strictly accountable according to His law?

11. THE TEN COMMANDMENTS AND THE DOUBLE COMMANDMENT

What does God desire of us? Does He want many things or only a few, or is just one thing needful? Doubtless He wants many things. Every moment He wants something different from us: that we should be stern with one man, mild with another; that, at one time we should yield, at another time be firm. He wants not only that we should not steal, but that we should be neither greedy nor covetous, not only that we give generously when we are moved to compassion, but also that we be frugal so that we may have wherewith to give. Also that we should not slander, judge, gossip, or speak unkindly. But neither does God approve of cowardly silence or tight-lipped selfishness when we might give counsel. Who can put down in detail just what God wants of us? Indeed we cannot think of a moment in our life when God wants nothing of us, nor of a moment in which He does not want something different than He wanted previously or may desire later, because each particular opportunity is unique and will never return. For that reason no one can ever retrieve what he has once let slip; each moment brings a new duty which wholly claims us. Life is like the endless chain in a modern factory; it passes by us and requires something particular every passing moment. It is not the nature of life itself but it is God who requires of us that we do *this* and not *that* to life as it passes by.

One can also say, on the other hand, that it is not many things which God requires,—but only a few; he gives us only a few commandments in which he says everything. He wants us to be conscientious in our words (9th Commandment). He wants us to deal justly with the affairs of other men, and respect the life of all (6th Commandment). He wants a right attitude toward those who are the only support of social order (5th Commandment). We are to respect not only the person but also the property of others (8th Commandment) etc. These fixed principles are the contents of the Ten Commandments. Everything that we should or should not do according to the will of God is contained therein.

It is also correct to say that we are simply to do one thing. He who keeps the first Commandment keeps all the rest. For the first Commandment means; thou shalt have *God* for thy God: which means that we should never forget, whatever we do, that we are not our own but God's property and must act accordingly. "Thou shalt love the Lord thy God with all thy heart." For only when you love God with all your heart do you really remember that you are His property, only then is it true for you that He is your God. All evil comes from our desire to be our own master, from loving ourselves more than God. Or, rather, it is not loving more, but loving falsely. To love oneself well one must love God, for it is only through love to God that we can achieve our true destiny.

God wants only that we should be that for which He

created us. He created us "in his own image." That is a simile. A man looks in the mirror and beholds his image, or some one shouts and the cliff echoes his cry. We have been created by God that we should reply to Him in the Word of Love with which He has called us into life. "Let us love him for he first loved us." That is *the* Commandment. All others are contained therein. But there is even more than the Commandment of God here. The Commandment of God is what God wants *of* us. But if we understand the words concerning the image of God, we also know what God wants *for* us. That God first loved us, before He demanded anything of us, and that He demands nothing more than that we should accept His love, that is, react to love with love, is simply what we call faith. Faith is the acceptance of God's grace, God's incomprehensible, undeserved Love; and whosoever does that fulfils the will of God.

Evil essentially is only the supposition that we can get along without God. This idea, "for my life God is superfluous: I am my own master," is the poisoning of the spring of human life; from this source all life is poisoned. The sin of Adam and Eve "ye shall be as Gods" does not mean to have the idea that one *is* God, but to endeavor to be independent *of* God. Free from God, away from God is to be God-less, evil. Against this all the Commandments are directed.

Haven't the Commandments more to do with men than with God? Are there two kinds of Commandments—those which tell us our duty to God and those which inform us of our obligations to man? Loving God and loving man? What does it really mean to love God? It means, as we have previously said, to know that all we have is from God; to know that God's goodness alone holds and supports us, and therefore to perceive that we belong absolutely to God. To know this banishes not only godlessness but also selfishness; and one is bound through God to his neighbor.

God gives us our life by giving us other men at the same time; He has so formed us that we cannot live alone. If things are right between ourselves and God, they are also right between ourselves and men. We look upon them as those to whom our life belongs. The man who knows himself to be God's property belongs thenceforth to his brethren. There is only one Commandment, it reduces at last to this—Love God and thy neighbor as thyself.

And now—on what terms are we with these Commandments? They are given us to do them. For what other purpose should they be given? Every man who has to do with God, knows that he should keep the Commandments at the cost of his life, if need be. But what man fulfils them? Do you really love God with all your heart and your neighbor as yourself? Because the first love is not true, neither is the other—and you lie, steal, commit adultery. Perhaps you do not break the Commandments in the gross sense of the word, but in the more refined and secret sense you do break them and you think that is not so bad? The more refined sins, under certain circumstances are much worse than the gross varieties. So then, we do *not* keep God's command. The spring of life *is* really poisoned, things *are* bad with us. This is the testimony of conscience and even more sharply and clearly, the testimony of Holy Scripture. Behind God's command stands the fearful word—Judgment! Lost! It is written more sharply in the New Testament than in the Old Testament. What then are we to do?

12. THE ORDINANCES OF GOD

Man is favored above the rest of creation in having a free will. "God created man in his own image"; he created man as a personal being, that is, as a being that does not simply develop of itself into that for which God created it, but rather as a being who achieves his destiny only by saying his "yes" to it. Children have dolls that say "yes," too. But they can say "yes" only when one presses them on the right spot; they can say neither yes nor no by their own decision or insight. They are automatons. Man is no automaton, he can and must continually decide how he is going to live. This capacity of deciding is the personal element in us, the free will.

Therein also lies, since we can freely decide for ourselves, our ability to do evil. An animal can do no wrong; it acts as it must, it has no freedom of choice. There are no good and bad rabbits, no good and bad foxes. They all do more or less the same, and have therefore neither a good nor a bad conscience. But men do not all act the same; each goes another way than the other, because each chooses his own way. Therefore no one is as the other. And yet the Apostle is right when he says "there is no difference, for all have sinned." This is so because every one chooses his own way, instead of God's way. There are as many individual ways as there are men, but there is only one way that is right, and that is God's way. And it is precisely this way which we do not follow—or are you perhaps the exception the Apostle overlooked, do you follow God's way?

But God in His creative goodness, having given man freedom to choose for himself, gave him something more in that when he sinned he might not wholly corrupt his life and the life of others, might not wholly deviate from God's way. This gift is the Ordinances of God. There are many things, despite our disloyalty, and wilfulness that come out right in our life, because God Himself has made it right. Thank God, we have no power over the change of seasons from summer to winter, over the course of the stars, no power over the laws of nature at work in our bodies. There are limits drawn about our lives by God's creative ordinance which we cannot trespass and within which, therefore, God's order prevails in spite of our sin.

There are, however, certain areas of God's creation where we can go out of bounds, but which limits we know ought not be transgressed. It is this I have in mind by the term, the Ordinances of God. Because they have been implanted in our nature by the Creator, every normal man has a kind of instinct for them, and yet they are ordinances lying within the realm of the will. The most important of these ordinances is the fact that God has so organized human life that no man can live for himself. He cannot live without the other. Man needs woman, woman needs man. The producer needs the consumer, the consumer the producer. The people need the leaders, the leaders need the people. Human life is so ordered by God because God has created man for love. Love is something voluntary, not even God can or will force it. But He does want to lead us in that direction. And so He has ordered life, that the individual can never take this direction without the aid of others. We are to be "exercised" so to speak, thereby, for love. It is because of the Ordinances of God that there is fellowship among men despite the dominating self-will which would wholly separate us.

However, just because man is intended to learn something by them, these Ordinances are no inviolable laws of nature, but can be disregarded by man. The more a man thinks of himself alone, and purposes for himself, so much the more are these Ordinances threatened with ruin. The more conscious man becomes of his ability to shape his own life, so much the more are these Ordinances of God endangered. And never in world history has that been more so than today. Every natural instinct for "what is fair," for those Ordinances that hold mankind together, is almost lost. The fellowship of man is consequently more and more dispersed. This can be most clearly noted in the marriage question. In earlier days people knew—even the heathen knew—that man and wife belonged together for life. Today that is no longer custom. Self-will begins to shatter even this most elemental Life Ordinance. In earlier days every one knew that children belonged to parents and parents to their children, the homogeniety of the family was taken for granted, but today it is threatened with collapse by the thought of self-sufficiency. In earlier days every one knew that there must be rulers and ruled, both needing each other but today every one wants to rule himself and take no advice.

Evil is present in every age, but it is not as predominant in one age as in another. Our day is in many respects better than earlier generations. But its difficulty and its evil consists in our no longer knowing the Ordinances of God, because every one wants to be "independent."

There has been selfishness in every age, but selfishness is today the recognized spirit because man no longer knows *that* God and *how* God created human beings for each other. Even the intellectual leaders of our time know it no more, for they think the highest achievement is to be a personality. But God has so formed life that one can become a personality only when he knows that he belongs to others and serves them. The man who recognizes nothing higher than reason becomes "independent"—he no longer needs others, he is his own master—even his own God. And then human fellowship is dissipated like a string of pearls when the cord is cut. What binds us together is the Ordinances of God, behind which stands God's love. He alone, who is bound to God and through God to his neighbor, can really become a man.

13. THE PROMISE

Every one has a bad conscience whenever he thinks about God, for we know quite well what God wants of us, and our own failure to do what He demands. We know that we are disobedient. But because we *know* that we do all the more what we ought not—we flee from God, we hide from Him like Adam and Eve after the Fall. The Law of God drives us away from God, or, more correctly, our bad conscience drives us away. We do not fear God, but we are afraid before God. Therefore the bad conscience, despite the fact that it tells us the truth, is, so to speak, an enemy of God. It is precisely this which stands between us and God. It does not let us come to God. A bad conscience and the law of God belong together. We have a bad conscience because we know the law of God. But the God who is known to us solely from the law is not at all the true God. The true God does not say first, "thou shalt," but "I am." How do the Ten Commandments begin? Not with "thou shalt have no other Gods before me," but with "I am the Lord thy God, which brought thee out of the land of Egypt, from the house of bondage."

God is not primarily the lawgiver, but the lifegiver. The essential is not what He demands but what He gives. As Creator He gives us life, the world with all its goods, his Ordinances are His gift. It is His gift that man and woman are created so wonderfully for each other, that the one can be happy only in the devotion to the other. Marriage is holy because it is God's gift. God does not give commands to show that He can give orders. His Commandments are nothing but explanations of his Ordinances which are gifts.

The meaning of all the Commandments is not to destroy that which God has so wondrously bestowed upon you—this life which is holy because it is God's gift; God's commandments are given to protect life from gross infringement, like a wall thrown about a glorious garden. The Commandments of God are gifts of God.

God wants to bestow more than this life upon us. Even the heathen know faintly that this life on earth is a gift of God the Creator. But they do not know that God wants to bestow something upon us much greater than life. This is the message of the Bible only. God did not say all at once what He proposed to give. His speaking begins with Abraham, "in thee shall all families of the earth be blessed." What this world-wide blessing of Abraham really is, Abraham does not know, but it is promised, and Abraham believed the word of promise. Later the Promise is of that wonderful King of righteousness and the kingdom of peace of which Isaiah prophesies: when righteousness will rule instead of unrighteousness, life instead of destruction, peace among the nations instead of war, peace even among the animals. The dawn becomes ever more bright. There comes Jeremiah with his God-given word of promise concerning a new covenant in which there will be not only righteousness and peace in the external sense of the word, but forgiveness of sin and peace with God, wherein the law of God will not have to be commanded, but goodness will be inscribed in the heart of man. And above all, God Himself will be graciously present with His people, and they shall really know themselves to be His people. Then finally, the clearness of morning before the sunrise, the New Testament in the midst of the Old, the promise of the coming servant of God, who takes upon himself the guilt of His people, bears their grief and through his suffering atones for the sin of man (Isaiah 53).

That is the biblical message, not what God wants *of* us, but what He desires *for* us; not what we should do, but what God does and gives. The *Law* of God is everywhere, the *Promise* of God is only in the Bible—the promise, namely, that God comes to His sick, rebellious people, to heal them, the message of the "Saviour," the healing, saving, forgiving, and redeeming God. This promise is really the Word of God.

Only so can one understand the Commandment of God aright. God desires nothing of us save that we allow Him to bestow life upon us, not merely this life that ends with death, but His life, that knows no death. To allow Him to give us life is nothing different than believing in Him, the saving, healing God. The beginning of the Ten Commandments can be rightly understood only from the fulfilment of the Promise: "I am the Lord thy God which brought thee out of the land of Egypt, from the house of bondage"—for what this house of bondage is and how God has led us forth from it, is revealed in the message of Jesus the Saviour-King, "Christ," the Saviour.

14. JESUS THE CHRIST

We speak of this age as the twentieth century. The year 1, the birth year of Jesus, divides world history in two parts—before Christ and after Christ. Thus the world acknowledges, externally at least, the coming of Jesus as the world epoch. One may well be amazed that so humble an event has had such tremendous universal consequences. And still all this is nothing, for it is possible that the calendar may be altered, and a new year accepted. Jesus as an epoch-making personality is —like all other world history—dust, mortality.

Who was Jesus? A great, saintly man, greater than all other saints? Founder of a religion, the greatest of all? The supreme example? If Jesus is that, then he is, like every other great man, dust. There will come a time when he will have nothing more to say to any one. Who was Jesus? As long as you ask in this way, you remain in a cool historical detachment from your question, quite interesting but fundamentally of no consequence. Ask, Who *is* Jesus? What is he to me? Can a man who lived nearly 2000 years ago mean anything to me? No! What was is past, and lives only through recollection. What was, does not, ultimately, concern you. For this reason he has two names—Jesus Christ. He is called Jesus for all who know him only through history. If you know him only so, he means nothing to you. *Jesus Christ* he is called for those to whom God reveals His own secret. Of ourselves we cannot give to Jesus the name *Christ*. Christ, Saviour, Redeemer, he is called only for him whom God Himself saves, through him. If we were to read in the paper tomorrow that a spring of quite wonderful properties had broken forth at Bethlehem, Palestine, and that whoever drank of this water would become healthy, what sort of a pilgrimage there would be to Bethlehem! "There alone healing is to be had," people would say. Yes, more than that has transpired, the divine spring has broken forth there, and whoever drinks of it "will never die—in eternity." How is that possible? What does that mean?

Jesus is a man, but in that human life something happened that never happened before. In him God's will, God's world plan, God Himself, whom we do not apprehend, but can merely surmise, became manifest. "He who sees me, sees the father." Jesus Christ is the sole "place" in the world where one can see God, and because we see God there, we also see ourselves anew —in truth. Of ourselves we do not know who we are; we do not rightly know what the Bible means in saying "God created man in his own image." Nor do we rightly know that we are sinners and lost creatures. Both can be known only when one knows God, but we do not know God. Who God is, and who we are, is revealed to us in Jesus Christ by God Himself. God had to come to us as man to show us ourselves, our own creation, and our own sin. But He came and showed us ourselves and Himself, to lead us from the lie unto the truth, from damnation to salvation, from perdition and death to life and blessedness.

God did not do this by setting up a picture, a mirage, a window—through which we could see into the heart of things, into the mystery of God and our own mystery. It is not as spectators that we can see Christ in Jesus, but only when we are challenged, called to an accounting, pressed to make a personal response, pressed for a decision. He alone apprehends Jesus as the Christ who allows God to call him in Christ. Before one answers yes to this call, one "sees" nothing—nothing but this remarkable man Jesus of Nazareth. When others say, he is the Saviour, the Redeemer that is of no significance to you, no more than a picture which some one else thinks beautiful should give *you* pleasure. You must know him yourself, be able to say yes to him. That is faith. Jesus is not the Christ for the onlooker, the thinker, the scholar, the historically informed, but simply and solely for the believer. "He that believeth in me, though he were dead, yet shall he live," he alone drinks from the spring of life.

It is proclaimed to all, behold the tabernacle of God is with men! Behold the Lamb of God that taketh away the sin of the world. Behold there, he, in whom God reveals your godlessness, and in spite of that, calls you His child! But the question is, whether we simply hear this message, or whether it finds the heart, whether we apprehend it as the truth, whether we hear God Himself come to us in Jesus calling us to Himself. When that happens Jesus is not simply Jesus of Nazareth, the great saint, but something happens to us as to Peter—

Verily thou art the Christ, the Son of the living God! Then will he also say to us, "blessed art thou, for flesh and blood hath not revealed it unto thee, but my Father in heaven." When that happens—Christmas has truly come.

15. THE SON OF MAN

Do you know what a man is? Is he not an abysmal riddle? What has the wholesale murderer of Düsseldorf in common with Father Bodelschwingh, or with Elizabeth Fry, the angel of the imprisoned? Which of those is "man," true man? One can say what a true fox, dog or eagle is—but what is a true man? Are *you* perhaps a true man? Really?

This question itself shows us at once the source of the riddle of man. It comes from our failure to be what we should be. Such a thing can be said only of man. He alone has freedom to be different than he ought to be. And indeed we are all different than we ought to be. What is written in the story of creation is no longer true, "God created man in his own image." We have all seen pictures taken in the World War, a man with helmet and gas mask, half erect and charging with fixed bayonet—the image of God? or the devil? Which does he most resemble? You could be this man! It is only "chance" that you or your husband, brother or son do not look like that. God's image? We recall the starving thousands in China, the pitiable folk in insane asylums, prisons, hospitals, the drunkard who is violent in his home, the prodigal son, wasting his substance in the far country, remembering that we, too, are this prodigal son who can say nothing more to his father than, "Father, I am no more worthy to be called thy son. . . ." What has happened to the image of God? Is it perhaps a fairy story? "You know what men are like. . . ." "I know something about men and know. . . ." Who can believe that fabulously great statement of the divine creation of man? A true man is an "ideal" that never occurs in reality. But how does it happen that we have such an ideal? How does it happen that every man knows quite well, I am no true man, things are not right with me? Whence this measure, this image of what we "really" ought to be? And whence the anxiety and the concern over our failure. When the Prodigal Son came to the extremity of his misery, keeping the swine, there awoke in him the memory of his home, and he sobbed with homesickness. How different it was at home! That is the secret experience of all of us. That "ideal" is like a yellowed photograph of us, "as we used to be." A faded picture scarcely visible any more; we can hardly believe that there is a "true man."

Here he stands before us, not a fantastic ideal, but a true man of flesh and blood. "Behold the man," the image of God. *That* is Jesus, man as God wanted him to be when He created him, the man who lives wholly in the things of his Father. "My meat is to do the will of him that sent me and to finish his work." He not only *says* it but *is* it in all the narratives and words that the Gospels report of him. The "Son of Man—" he, before whom one must halt and say, yes, I have found him whom I have been seeking—the man, the true Man.

What does it profit us that he lived 1900 years ago? For all of that we are not what we ought to be. But this man Jesus has something to say to us. "I am sent to you by my father—by your father, to tell you that He wants to make you like me. You are to become as truly man as I am."

"Who, me?"

"Yes, you!"

"But that is impossible—I'm a poor sort of man; no one can make anything much out of me."

"You are right. No one can do it but God. But He will."

Jesus Christ is come not only to show us the true man, but to tell us God's purposes to remake us in our lost image. That you shall become. Moreover, you shall be like Jesus Christ, who has gone into eternity. "It doth not yet appear what we shall be: but we know that, when he shall appear, we shall be like him."

That is the glad message of the Gospel. We suffer most from ourselves, even when we do not realize it, even when we suppose the cause of our grief and suffering is from without. The deepest cause of all that is not right, is that we ourselves are not right. And therefore that is the greatest message that we can hear—things will be right with you. Ponder how a blind man must feel when he is told, "You will receive your sight again," or when a cripple is told, "You will be straight and strong again!" And this is only external! We are to become internally right again, straight and strong and fine through God's grace. "Rejoice with exceeding joy." That is the message of the Son of Man.

16. THE SON OF GOD

No man can know who God is. The cleverest scholar

knows nothing more concerning God than the simplest man. There dwells of course within every human heart a feeling of something higher than itself, a dim apprehension of a Power ruling all that is, and giving His Law to all that lives. But how dark and confused this presentiment is, is shown by the history of mankind and by everyday life. What variety of ideas men have of "God" and "the divine"—and how many have no conception of the matter whatsoever. Who dare to say, "I know who God is. I know His plans and purposes?" This much we know of God; He is the great mystery. And we know something else, even though obscurely—that things are not well between God and ourselves. We cannot dismiss either one, the darkness surrounding God, and the darkness in ourselves. Can it be that both are the same?

"No man hath seen God at any time; the only begotten Son, which is in the bosom of the Father, he hath declared Him." Why did the Apostles and the first Christians call Jesus the Son of God? Because in him they discovered who God is. Jesus is like God. To be enabled to perceive that Jesus was not simply a noble, engaging man but the manifestation of the nature of God was the crisis and creative moment of their faith;

and that perception was the glad news. In him God speaks to us. Therefore the first Christians also called him the Word of God. The Prophets were called of God and commissioned to proclaim the Word of God. But what they spoke was not yet the real Word of God. It was but the Prophet who spoke, not God Himself. They were His tools, mouthpieces, but He Himself remained hidden and far away. No prophet had the temerity to say, look at me, and then you will know who God is.

Still the Prophets had something which no one else in all the history of the world possessed—neither the great Chinese sages, nor the Greek philosophers, nor the saints of India. They had a message from God Himself. The Prophets *had* indeed the Word of God; but they themselves *were* not the Word. Hence they knew that something greater was yet to come; they pointed to the future, to the coming Messiah. Even the last of the Prophets, John the Baptist, spoke so. "But One mightier than I cometh, the latchet of whose shoes I am not worthy to unloose, . . ." He, who is more than a prophet!

Who is more than a prophet? One who not only *has* the Word, but *is* the Word! He who does not merely proclaim and promise salvation, but gives it. He who unlike the Prophets does not need to be told of God what to say, but who speaks of God as of Himself, who possesses within himself the fountainhead of the Word of God, who does not stand awe-stricken before the mystery of God, but who, himself, reveals the mystery of God. No man can be that. Man can never be more than a prophet. Above the prophet stands only the One who Himself equips the prophet, who gives the Word—God. God alone possesses the Word, and no one can say, the Word of God comes from me, except God. He who says, Jesus is more than a prophet, Jesus is the Word of God—says, Jesus is not simply a man like us, but he is God Himself.

That is the inconceivable—and precisely in this inconceivable subsists the Christian faith. Non-Christians have everything but this, they have the commandments of God, even the commandment to love one's neighbor, the omnipotence and wisdom of God. But this they do not have—God, who Himself comes to us and shows Himself to us as God-man, longs for fellowship with us, and that He—in spite of all—is not ashamed of us, but loves us and desires to bring us to glory.

This God, who condescends to man and comes so

near the humankind as though He were one of them—this God the heathen do not have. And we know this God only because of what has happened. This self-condescension, this humiliation, this God we have in Jesus Christ.

To be sure not every one has God in Jesus Christ. All depends on what Jesus means to a man. He to whom Jesus is only a man—were he ever so exalted, pious, noble, wise, the greatest of all religious founders and saints—does not have this God. "He who hath not the Son, hath not the Father." It is with him as with a man who has a banknote on which is printed 1000 dollars; the belief that the note is counterfeit makes it worthless to such an one, a mere scrap of paper. He does not have the 1000 dollars. He who does not believe that in Jesus God Himself comes to us, does not apprehend the God who reveals Himself to us in the coming of Jesus Christ. He does not perceive the gracious will of God; God's secret, the divine plans for the world are not unveiled for him. The atonement did not take place for him; Jesus Christ is not God's word and deed for him. He is not that man's Saviour. For a man cannot save us. Only God can do that, only Jesus Christ can do that if God is in him as the Saviour.

We should honor great men, saintly men are noble examples for us, but no great or saintly man can reveal God's mystery to us and bind us with God; no man can take away our guilt and make us certain of the completion of life in eternal life. This God alone can do, and He does just that in Jesus Christ, who, for that reason is not merely a great man, but the Son of God. How does it happen that God comes to us as man? I do not know, I do not even know how it happens that something becomes alive, that a man is born. That is God's secret as Creator. How much more the incarnation of God remains His secret. But what I can know, and what I can rejoice in every day as a Christian is that God bestows His love upon me in His Son, and that He will give it to all who believe on him, the Son of God.

17. THE KING

It is especially difficult for Swiss people to believe that we must and do have a king. The word Liberty was sung to us even in the cradle. It is a beautiful word, and we rightly exalt it. But this honor of liberty is only one half of the truth, liberty is not the first, but the second word. The first word is obedience. God created man *in His own image*—which means that we are created for liberty. But we have overlooked the first word: *God* created man. Therefore God is master. As long as men keep that firmly in mind, that God is Lord, they may and should strive for liberty; but when they have forgotten the primary truth their liberty becomes license and arrogance. What is true of the child is true also of adults. We become free only through obedience. A child who has never been obliged to follow, remains a weak creature all his life, the football of his moods, a slave of his desires and passions. A man who holds aloft only the one word Liberty without knowing first and foremost that God is the Lord, whom man must unquestioningly obey, is and remains a child, a spoiled, poor, silly child. The most important word in our language is the one so often thoughtlessly and profanely used—Lord God. The fear of the Lord is the beginning of wisdom. That is the undergirding of a sound house. Where the foundation is weak or decayed the house is constantly threatened with collapse. How much more important is this solid base than a good coat of paint on the weather boarding outside.

God, the Creator of all things, your Creator and mine, desires to rule, to be king. But He does not propose to be a tyrant. He could do with us what He would; He could so make us that we were unable to do wrong, like a machine that performs what it was made to do and nothing else.

God, however, does not want that! He does not want us to be machines, He does not want us to be compelled to do His will, but that we might do it of our own free will. And that means obedience, for only he who freely does the will of God, of his own accord, really obeys; all other obedience is pretense for it does not come from the heart. God wants us to obey Him with all our heart, in reverence and love. Such a king He desires to be. For this cause He has sent us Jesus Christ, for this reason He has given us the Gospel. The Gospel is the message of the "Kingdom" of God,—more correctly the "reign" of God.

Who is God, where is God? God is in heaven, people say, and that is far away. God is invisible, unknown—and so obedience is difficult. No doubt the great house of God, the world in which we live is full of traces of the Lord who built it and to whom it belongs, but He himself, the King, we do not meet in His house. And we want to meet Him, not His works only but—Him, His very self. The Prophets of the Old Testament brought indeed messages of this royal Lord, like heralds whom the king sends to proclaim his will. And they were permitted to say something more. They proclaimed that He Himself was coming soon and would no longer be distant, but would dwell with His people. He comes, He comes, He Himself! So could they speak because they saw Him coming, He in whom the invisible God was visible, the distant and inconceivable one was near and conceivable, yet they never saw Him upon earth. But like the servant who announces the king's coming, they draw back the curtain and say, this is He —so John the Baptist, the last Prophet, proclaimed at the coming of the Lord, The Lord! Here He is—*He Himself.*

That is our Lord Jesus Christ. Hence the kingdom of God begins with him, the time of the reign of God. "He came unto his own." The will of God, the mystery of God, the heart of God, the hidden counsels of God are revealed in Jesus Christ. God comes as a *man* to the sons of men for only so could men understand Him. God in heaven—is something so distant, pale and indefinite that He scarcely concerns us at all. God in heaven causes us no concern. But the conception of God on earth is something serious for it brings the will of God near and unavoidable, as clear and perceptible as the will of a man we meet. The Jews felt indeed this crisis and that is why they wanted to have nothing to do with him. They killed him. It transpired exactly as the Lord prophesied in his Parable of the Vineyard (Matt. 21). The husbandmen themselves crave Lordship, so they murder the messengers who come to collect the rent; they murder the Lord's son who comes to restore the property to his Father.

So, too, do we. We want to be our own Lords. "He came unto his own and his own received him not." Jesus Christ is come but we will not have him for our king, we want to remain "free." But that simply means we want to remain slaves of evil, for if Christ does not reign in us, some one else does. Evil desire, greed, covetousness, thirst for honor, thirst for power, egotism. One can believe that these things comprise freedom. In reality they are slavery, and this can be demonstrated by the results—unhappiness and the creation of unhappiness. Men thus enslaved become *in-human,* evil, and society becomes a strife of man against man. There is neither peace within nor with other men, for God has ordained that man shall be forever peaceless, joyless, in bondage, except in obedience to the Creator. "But as many as received him to them gave he power to become the sons of God." Thank God the story of the husbandmen need not be repeated. It can happen that a man accepts Jesus as his king. Just that is faith. Faith does not consist in self-made opinions about the Bible and God, nor in accepting the opinions of other people. Faith means to accept Jesus as King and obey him. That is the oldest creed of the Christian Church —Jesus, the Lord! This confession, of course, may be a mere phrase, a surface opinion. But then it is a lie. For "My Lord" means him whom I obey. Faith is obedience, and the Christian life, is, so to speak, military service: marching under the command of Jesus, the Lord. But quite different from the army, too! The command is the will of him who allowed himself to be killed on a cross, that we might learn the meaning of obedience, of sacrifice in service to one's neighbor.

18. THE MEDIATOR

The power of evil is in our guilt. Having erred we cannot make our wrong good, henceforth we have no power over it. Our evil now belongs to the past, it is now written yonder in eternity. As every mile a man drives in his car is automatically registered upon the speedometer, so everything we do is somehow "registered" in eternity, to appear for the first time on the Judgment Day. As soon as a thing is done, it is recorded, and no repentance can alter the record in the slightest degree. It stands there and testifies against us —guilty!

This "register" in the realm of eternity has, moreover, another uncomfortable feature. It not only registers what men see in me, but what God sees in me. Like the X-ray that reveals the inner parts that otherwise remain invisible, God looks upon the heart. *Thy* heart, O man! Does that not frighten you? Does that not cause despair? "For in thy sight, Lord, shall no man living be justified." Make no mistake about it, on that register is written our death sentence. When God makes up the account, there can be no other statement than— unfaithful! unfaithful! cast out!

That is what conscience tells us. In these days conscience seems to judge less severely. Who in our time ever thinks of Hell, or of being lost? Old wives' tales! We understand how to manipulate the register so that nothing causes us alarm. But such manipulation with the conscience really profits nothing. The register in eternity still shows the judgment—lost. Conscience still informs us secretly—thou hast not taken God's will in earnest. Thou canst not stand in His judgment. And secretly every one feels this. There is no one who does not fear God—even those who deny God and laugh at faith in God. Beneath the surface, deep down in the soul, dwells the fear of God, the fear of being lost. Our conscience tells us that; it is—as Paul expressed it once, "the handwriting . . . against us" (Col. 2:14); such is the meaning of the word guilt.

What does God say to all this? He tells us that the voice within speaks truly. The conscience that accuses us does not lie. That meter, upon which our guilt mounts like the mileage of the automobile, is God's instrument. We said that conscience registers what God sees, what God says. In God's chancery the death sentence against us is made up.

"Yes, but. . . ." Have we any right to say "Yes, but"? Is it possible that God "may not be so strict," and, as the saying is, "may stretch a point in our favor"? The judgment, "the handwriting against us" is finished and signed by God. But. . . .

But, Jesus Christ, the crucified hath "forgiven you all trespasses; blotting out the handwriting of ordinances that was against us . . . and took it out of the way, nailing it to his cross." Not as though the sentence of death were meaningless. Registered means surely that from our point of view we are guilty and lost. Precisely this is what God wants to tell us by the cross of His Son. God will not wink at evil, He takes our guilt seriously. Even for Him it is nothing inconsiderable. He cannot and will not tear up the "manuscript." He could no doubt do so, but for our sakes He will not. For we should then take guilt too lightly, and God desires to show us that what is written on the manuscript is correct. He will even carry out the judgment. But . . . over all stands His forgiving father love.

He will not destroy the manuscript that testifies against us, but He will destroy its power by a higher power. He has "nailed it to the cross" that we might see both our guilt and His even greater mercy; the earnestness of His holy will and the even greater earnestness of His fatherly love. That is the message of Jesus Christ, the Mediator.

Suppose a farmhand set fire to his master's barn. The man is liable for the damages with all that he has. The master could take everything the servant has—shoes, clothing, money, and say, "All of this is only a small part of what my servant really owes me. And now let the scoundrel get out of my sight!" But the master does nothing of the sort, takes nothing away. He rather says to his faithless servant, "I will take everything upon myself; I will pay everything." And then the servant opens his eyes in amazement; for he sees what a good master he has.

God dealt with us in this way through Jesus Christ. He has taken everything upon Himself; He has Himself borne the curse of sin that we should have carried. Jesus went to the cross, because man could not have endured the presence of God. In permitting himself to be crucified Jesus both brought God nearer, and himself showed man more clearly his distance from God. The manuscript that testifies against us, is there displayed, legible to all, our death sentence. And at the same time it is destroyed, God loves you in spite of all. God's son had to go through this shambles really to come near to us. All this was necessary that we men might see God and ourselves, God in His love, and ourselves in our godlessness. Apart from the cross on Golgotha we should know neither our condition nor the boundlessness of God's love. God and man can there be seen together—human misery and perdition, and God's presence and ineffable love. Jesus reveals both us and God on the Cross. And by that act he accomplishes the greatest thing possible: he brings man back again to God.

He accomplishes "the atonement through his blood." As a mother follows her lost child in all its misery, filth and shame, so, too, God in Jesus Christ came into our condition to be wholly with us. Thus Jesus, the crucified, is the promised "God with us" or "Immanuel" and Golgotha the one place in all the world where we may behold the mystery of divine Love. Who—we? I will say it more correctly—*you,* if you permit God to tell you by name that this was done because you need it, and because God loves you.

19. THE HOLY GHOST

Many a person has opened the Bible at some time or other, turned over a few pages, read this and that, and laid it aside again, saying, "Nothing there for me." Perhaps a few years later, after something has happened to him, he has read the same passages again. But now every word is like a hammer blow of God upon his heart. Why this difference? One can express it in two ways, from the human side and from the divine side. One can say that the Lord opened the heart as was said of that seller of purple (Acts 16); or one can say that God's spirit spoke directly through the Bible.

Without the work of God's spirit in opening our hearts, we cannot really understand the Bible. The book may appear interesting, or instructive, or touchingly beautiful to us; but to move the heart so that we know that God is now speaking to us, Himself to myself, this the Bible can do only when the Holy Spirit is added. So too is it with the message of the preacher on Sunday: we can hear a fine sermon without the Holy Spirit, but we then do not hear the Word of God in the sermon. Even a simple man on the street or at home can speak the Word of God to us—through the Holy Spirit.

God has not spoken only in past times by the Prophets and Apostles. He speaks today. But not everything that pretends to be the Word of the Holy Spirit is what it claims to be. We need a measure by which to know what is of the Spirit of God and what is not. This measure is the Bible, the document, the original word of the Holy Spirit, the normal meter upon which all that claims to be God's Word must be gauged. Whatever fails to agree with it, cannot be God's Word.

The Holy Spirit does not only *speak.* When God really speaks there occurs not empty words but action. God's Word is ever the Word of the Creator. The Holy

Spirit is creative power, wonder—might. When God's Spirit enters a life, something miraculous always takes place. All becomes different than before. The letters of the Apostle are full of the miraculous workings of the Spirit of God. The first and perhaps most important is the fact that the human heart formerly disquieted, divided, rebellious, and at the same time despairing, becomes peaceful. "Peace with God," "reconciled" is the apostolic description. We are by nature at war with God and consequently at war, too, with man. We are not in a position to bring peace out of this conflict. The most wonderful thing that can happen to a man in this earthly life is to become right with God. The immediate result is joy. Many men claim they believe in God, but they go through life with as little peace as those who believe nothing. So to live is to manifest a misunderstanding of what belief means. A man who has really found God, so that God Himself has spoken to him and said, "You are my child," cannot be disquieted any more; a great never-ceasing joy has been kindled in him. This joy can almost be smothered by life's ashes, but it cannot be quenched. It continues to break forth again and again in spite of the ashes, and that is the work of the Holy Spirit.

The greatest fruit and the most glorious miracle is

love. Love is an inward openness to the needs of others. As long as we do not love, the "other" remains on the outside. He is locked out, a stranger. We are for ourselves, and the "other's" existence has significance only as it pertains to ourselves. Love is a miracle that makes of the "other" no stranger; we are created for him, here for him, ready for him, eyes and ears for him; our whole being speaks to him—come in, you are welcome here! An open door for my neighbor is love, the greatest miracle of the Holy Spirit.

The Spirit of God renews men. We say of ourselves, I am as I am; as we say of another, he is as he is. We mean that each man receives this or that nature from his parents, and lives his life true to his received endowment. We say that as surely as an apple cannot be changed to a pear, so surely is a person's nature unalterable. But He who made the apples and pears, the Creator, can alter anything and He does it, too. The Bible is full of the message of transformation. "If any man is in Christ he is a new creature; old things are passed away, behold, all things are become new." That is the miracle of the Holy Spirit.

In the New Testament the Holy Spirit is in an especial manner the Spirit of the "community" of Jesus, the

"Church." For the Holy Spirit is a spirit of fellowship, bringing individuals out of their isolation, making "one body" of them. To be sure there is for the most part little evidence of this in our churches, a sign of how little the Holy Spirit is alive within them. As the fire is to be known by its brightness and warmth, so the Spirit of God is to be known by the fellowship it produces. And as fire kindles fire (what looks like fire but does not spread is probably only pyrotechnical display), so life kindled by the Holy Spirit must spread and ignite all with its burning. It was in this way that the Church of Jesus Christ spread, it was in this way that the Reformation set all Europe on fire within a few years. It is the Spirit's way of working. The Holy Spirit is God at work now, redeeming, coming to us in the word concerning His Son, the "triune" God.

20. FAITH OR DESPAIR

"It is enough to drive one to despair!" We have all uttered these words when we have waited vainly for the success of a cherished project, when great and repeated exertions have not caused our work to prosper, when our high expectations of another person have not been fulfilled. Fortunately these dismal moods do not come every day, for if they did we should indeed be driven to despair.

There are people, however, who have the feeling of despair, not now and then but constantly, and when we observe carefully we realize that there are more such folk than we are apt at first to think. We are often desperate without noting it or knowing why. *Why* do we despair, really? We are driven to despair when there is apparently no way out, no goal in view. But do we *see* the way out, the goal? One goal we certainly see—death. We must all go hence, is that not enough to drive us to despair? If death terminates all—can there be anything more desperate than that? No other goal, no way out, no sense to anything, everything in vain, if the close of all things is always the one vast empty nothing. Death—the great chasm into which all must eventually fall, the beautiful along with the dissolute, the good along with the bad, the valuable and the valueless alike. When a lad in the first grade has taken great pains with his drawing only to have the teacher snatch it roughly out of his hand, tear it to bits and throw the pieces into the wastebasket—isn't that enough to drive the poor little lad to despair? But are we not all such poor little fellows, whose teacher is death, casting into the great chasm with his rough hand all that we have created, all that we have tended and built up with loving care? Does that not make us desperate?

There is only one thing more fearful than the thought that death ends all: that one is in such dreadful condition that he hopes that death ends all, because he is fearful of what is to come afterward. When a bad conscience troubles a man so that he must think: I will be punished for what I have done; there will come a day when all things will appear in the light of day, the great unavoidable reckoning. When one is so desperate that death—I mean death as the ultimate—seems a way out, a goal to be desired—that is the ultimate desolation. Whether or not we give this most fearful thing the name Hell is of no significance; the name does not matter. This thought, in any case, leads one to despair. And who has never had such a thought? Have you so lived that you can be sure it does not await *you?* Are you certain this is not your goal? Death and Hell as a goal is indeed enough to drive one to despair, and who or what can free us from utter dejection? No one, nothing can do it. For no one can avert death, and no one can take away my guilt. All the lovely, charming, and powerful things of life cannot master this despair. Who is master over death and the fear of Hell? You can determine not to think about it—draw the curtains of your soul. You can plunge into work, to forget it, you can drown your sorrow in drink, plunge into society and gossip in order to drown out these voices of despair—but it is useless. When children at play try to stop the flow of a spring by placing their hands over the overflow pipe, the water spurts out from under their fingers. So, too, with the resolution not to think about our despair. We become ill and nervous, sleep badly, discover desires unknown before, in short our despair works within the deep and dark places of our being like a sinister and destructive spirit. To dismiss conscious thoughts of our despair is not to cure it. How, how shall we come to terms with this thing?

There is but one word strong enough to conquer despair—and that is faith. Either we despair—or we believe. Nothing but faith is able to swallow up despair, there is no other alternative. That is the great either-or in life, more important than any other. Either despair—or faith. That means that either everything will come out all right, or everything will come out all wrong. Either death and Hell in the end, or the end is

God. Faith means with all things end in God. "Death is swallowed up in victory. O death, where is thy sting, O grave, where is thy victory? Thanks be to God who giveth us the victory . . ." So to speak is the work of faith. Only he who believes in God wins the victory over despair.

Who can speak that way: ". . . who hath *given* us the victory?" Who is able to say, We *have* the victory? Death and Hell *are* overcome for us? Who has spoken this glorious word and how could he do it? Listen to the rest of the quotation: "Thanks be to God who giveth us the victory through our Lord Jesus Christ." That is the victory; Jesus Christ is *the* Word of God, *the* Word with which God robs death and Hell of their power to make us despair. God in Christ has closed the chasm of death and quenched the flames of Hell—for every one that believes on Him. For: "he that believeth on me, though he were dead, yet shall he live." "For I am persuaded, that neither death nor life, nor principalities, nor powers . . . (nothing) shall be able to separate us from the love of God which is in Christ Jesus our Lord." Hence we must constantly keep Jesus Christ before us. Because he is the Victory, because in him God forgives our guilt, and because in him God promises us eternal life. Faith means to hear Jesus as God's Word to us, and see him as God's victory; and that alone means the end of despair.

21. BY FAITH ALONE

"By faith alone" was the battle cry of the Reformation. Can it, must it retain its priority today? Moreover, is it not a dangerous, even a false slogan? Has not this slogan become a challenge to polemical battle? Has it not produced among Christians the false idea that it depends "only" on the correctness of one's faith, and minimizes the correctness of one's life? If this is what one understands by "faith" the taking for granted of certain dogmas, the simple acceptance of what is in the Bible as true—there is indeed no more fatal error in Christianity than the saying "by faith alone." Faith then is a certain viewpoint, a *weltanschauung,* side by side with other theories and ideas. But a theory or a world-view, be it Christian or another, can never be essential. What does God ask about our theories or ideas? What does God care whether we have the "Christian world-view" or another! The spectator who strolls through life, has a viewpoint for he does not engage in the battle. God forbids us to be idlers, he wants fighters.

It is only from the thick of the fight that one can understand what the Reformers and the Apostles meant by the word "faith." What do you "believe" rightly understood means, whom do you trust, to whom have you pledged your loyalty? Or it means what we were perhaps asked as children, whose child are you? That I belong wholly to God, that I, as the Heidelberg catechism so beautifully expresses it, "with body and soul, both in life and in death, am not my own, but belong to my faithful Saviour Jesus Christ . . . and makes me heartily willing and ready henceforth to live unto Him."

Just as it is false to confuse faith with a viewpoint, a mere acceptance of certain "dogmas," so, too, it is wrong to suppose that faith is only a vague "trust in God" which even the pious heathen have also possessed. Why then would we need the Bible, the Revelation of God in Jesus Christ, the Cross and his Resurrection? It certainly depends upon trusting the true God and not any sort of chimera of the divine; that we entrust ourselves to the God who revealed Himself in Jesus Christ and nowhere else as our true, real God, and not simply to a product of our fantasy. When one takes the word "faith" seriously, as it is meant in the Bible, a man cannot truly believe in any other God than Him who in Jesus Christ has shown Himself to us and called us to Himself. One believes truly only when one knows "by faith alone" and the pious heathen know nothing of that. The Bible alone speaks of this "by faith alone." Why is that?

Pious heathen of ancient and modern times all want to come to God themselves, by prayer, by a virtuous life, by stern discipline, by a holy life. They think, that if they are earnest enough about this pious life, that they are true to God, and He will accept them. All pious heathenism—even all pious "Christian" heathenism—is "righteousness by the works of the law," trust in what man does. But in contrast to this the Bible says that you cannot be "good enough." If you choose to go this way, there are only two possibilities: either you deceive yourself about yourself, forgetting that you are a sinful man, confusing the demands of God with the standards of middle-class integrity and thus satisfying yourself; or you really take God's will seriously and fall into despair when you see that you can never be just before that will. Frequently it happens then that the pendulum swings back and forth between false self-trust and despair. That is the religion of the pagan. In the Bible, however, it is said that you cannot satisfy God, but God satisfies Himself and you. You are not to rely on what you do, but solely, alone on what God does. We must say even more than that. You cannot know what the word "God" means until you are at the end of your strength, and can hope only in God. The man who has not yet discovered this "God only" has not yet discovered God. The gods of the heathen are not truly God. The true God is the God one finds when he can no longer help himself, and he puts his hope in Him alone. To hope in God alone, not in the power of self, one's ability or knowledge, means faith, means being God's own.

This is harder than all penances, prayers, and the good works of the pious heathen. For there is nothing in all the world so humiliating as no longer to trust in one's self. And nothing is so difficult in all the world as to trust in God alone. Difficult? Indeed—Impossible! We cannot force our being's abdication and accept God alone. Only God can do that for us. And he *has* done that for us—on the Saviour's cross. It is there that a double action is accomplished, for our pride is broken and buried—and there God comes to meet us, He who *alone* can help. To believe aright means, then to receive the crucified Christ, to apprehend in his cross the end of all our self-redeeming activity, and the beginning of God's creative redemption. That God alone can and does help—this is closed to our knowledge, inaccessible to our trust except through the cross of Christ. "By faith alone" then, means not I, but God alone creates my redemption, my salvation, the saving and redeeming of the world; He alone is good, He alone brings to the desired goal—"with might of ours can naught be done;"—that means to rely on God alone, to make God our whole defense.

Does not that make man lazy? Ask a Luther, a Zwingli, a Calvin whether this "God alone" faith made *them* lazy! Examine the lives of others who have really received this "God alone" faith in all of its depth and magnificence, and inquire whether it has made them morally indifferent or ethically lazy. It is the great mystery of God that men do not become strong until they know their weakness, and expect all things from the power of God. The strong, the real "doers" in Christendom have been those who relied solely on the work of God, and not those who trusted much in human activity. For God's power is made perfect in weakness, and only when a man knows how weak he is can God become mighty in him. It is precisely the truly good that is done "by faith alone."

22. CONVERSION

There are reasons for our dislike of the word Conversion; it has done and still does much mischief. We all know of particularly devout persons who pounce upon their amazed fellow men at work, on the street, in the street-car with the sudden question, Tell me, are you converted? This is not the manner and method of the New Testament. Jesus went through the villages and towns of Galilee, and cried, "Repent, for the Kingdom of God is at hand." That the Christian life must be a daily repentance or conversion, was the first of Luther's Ninety-five Theses, with which the Reformation began. A man who does not know what repentance is, does not know the meaning of faith, forgiveness, or Jesus Christ. What, then, is repentance?

A right about face—something as astonishing as though the water of the Rhine River should suddenly start flowing upstream instead of downstream. The natural "inclination" of our heart and will is to seek ourselves. Like the rapacious spider that sits in the center of his web, we sit in the midst of our world in a spirit of acquisitiveness. We want men and what men have, their happiness, their possessions, their honor, their power. All this is our booty. But we want also from men their love, their respect, their time, and their sympathy. Our Ego sits like a king enthroned and demands that the world serve it. My wife, my children, my school, and—yes, even my dear God, are all to serve "me." *I* am the Lord my God. Some maintain this primacy of the ego with delicacy, others coarsely; but all maintain it. So is the natural man, the unconverted man, the godless, loveless man. If any believes that I have made too harsh a judgment let him speak for himself. I confess in any case that *I* am such a man, —and those I know are such people.

Something can happen in this sphere, however, that never happens in nature. The water of a stream never flows uphill, a goose never becomes a fox, or a fox a goose. But it can, moreover it does happen, that this natural "inclination" of the human heart to say "I, I" can be reversed so that it says instead "Thou, Thou." That is the great miracle, the miracle that we designate with the word Love. Love is simply this, that one no longer sits, like the spider, in the midst of its web, or ke the King Ego upon his throne, demanding service, but that one instead of living for himself, lives for others, instead of ruling, serves. There was one who could say of himself, "I am not come to be ministered unto but to minister." That was the decisive event in all human history: Jesus Christ who gave his life a ransom for many and his blood for the forgiveness of sin. Hence we know and the world knows because he came, what Love is.

Through him it is possible for the first time that this so new and totally different spirit becomes effective in the lives of others, for through Christ, God becomes the center about which everything revolves. He who is the sole legitimate king of our life, now becomes King in reality. He ascends the throne previously occupied by the pretender king, Ego, a truly violent revolution. And this revolution, (*Umwälzung*), is called in the Bible, repentance, return, conversion. When God becomes King, it happens that instead of "I, I" one says "Thou, Thou." This "thou" is addressed in the first place and primarily to God. "Thou God art my Lord." But whoever comes to God experiences something noteworthy. At His door one hears the words, Go forth yonder where "thy neighbor" lives. God directs you with your love to your neighbor. You are to serve him.

That is your reasonable worship. You are to show by your love to your neighbor whether you really love God.

This, then, is conversion: that we seek first the Kingdom of God; that God's desire, namely, service to our neighbor, becomes our chief concern. But you cannot convert yourself; God alone can do it. He does it by addressing you both as your Judge and as your Redeemer, as He who "forgiveth all thine iniquities and healeth all thy diseases." And this conversion takes place within you whenever you permit God to say to you what He wants to say to you.

This reception of God's earnest voice happens, indeed, for a first time; and in that sense one may speak of "my conversion." But it is more deeply true that one must be converted anew each day. Perhaps you bear in memory the time when it first happened; but there are many who cannot be definite about the "first time" who nevertheless know that it *has* happened, and happens every day. But there is another possibility, perhaps it has *never* happened to you! In that event that seemingly arrogant question, "Are you converted?" is, indeed, not so improper after all. But the man who is really converted, that is, in whom conversion is a daily happening, and not an isolated moment, will not arrogantly parade his conversion. But he will long for every neighbor of his, that the other may share the life that he has received.

23. REGENERATION

None can understand the mystery of birth. The physician can "explain" how it comes about, and we can follow his "explanation." But as soon as we cease talking about the "something that originates in this way" and halt to think of ourselves as we know ourselves, what appeared as an explanation shows the face of a yet deeper mystery. "My life—what does it really mean? Once I did not exist, I was born, now I am here, alive!" Such thoughts quiet all "explanations" and permit only that we marvel and say, "I cannot understand it at all." And yet, our quietness brings us before the fundamental question of existence. Our life is lived between two darknesses, the mystery of birth and the mystery of death. Birth means, "Here I am, I do not know why. I am what I am, I do not know why." And this, "Here I am as I am" cannot be spoken in the same manner as the words of the little lad who runs happily into the room, up to his mother, crying "Here I am!" Our words cannot be spoken thus, so happily, so simply, in so matter of fact a manner. We cannot say this "Here I am" and "As I am" without hearing something sigh within us,—something of the feeling of a man who is hailed into police court or thrown into prison, and who now examines his cell, hurt, rebellious, sad, anxious. "*Here* I am—why, really?" This question is concealed in every heart, but we scarcely note how it troubles us. We do not understand it.

Now, however, the cell door opens and we are told why *our* "Here I am, as I am" is so sad, anxious, and incomprehensible. God's Word tells us the secret of our life, created of God art thou, in His image, fallen from God hast thou, into sin! The Word of God, Jesus Christ gives you understanding of the meaning both of God's creation and our sin. When? How? We shall never understand this as long as we live, all we now know is, as far back as we can remember both have been present: that which comes from God and that which is against God, creation and sin. Already at the time a child is born both have had their share; they reach far back into the ancestry of the child, and all who are human beings have this double ancestry. Furthermore, the Gospel tells us that we are not only unhappy in this state but that in it we are cut off and lost from real life and from the truly good.

The Word of God says, secondly, that God pities us, that He saves us, the lost creation. He, against whom we live, is for us; he, without whom we live, comes to us. In Jesus Christ is given the double word—God's inconceivable forgiveness and His promise of complete renewal. He shows us a picture totally different from what we see in ourselves. It is a picture of man truly, and perfectly undistorted, God's image. Whose picture is that? Your picture, says Christ—it is you, through God's grace. God gives you this when you permit Him to draw you really and wholly to Him, when you believe and trust Him with all your heart.

When that happens, when a man really listens to God Himself, to Jesus Christ Himself—what then? The Bible replies to this "what then?" with the word *regeneration.* Something has then taken place just as powerful and inconceivable as birth, the saying "Here I am as I am" finds a new meaning. "If any man is in Christ he is a new creature, old things are passed away, behold all things are become new." The old man still remains visible, but under the husk of the old, lives the new and begins to discard the old. Something visible begins to break forth from the invisible faith. It is love, a new manner of life, thought and speech, a new way of dealing with one's neighbor. It is not as though the old man simply disappeared, yet however a new life appears in transformations that give those, who know nothing of faith, something to think about and perhaps to ask about. Why has he changed so?

Do such things really happen? Or is this just a beautiful fantasy? No, says the Bible, there are such new men, whether they have names like Paul or Timothy, or, whether like the Philippian jailor, their names are unknown. Such renewal is to be found not only in the New Testament, but ever since then in every place where the Word of God concerning Jesus Christ is really believed "with the heart, not merely with the head" as Calvin says,—wherever a son of man is bound anew with the heavenly Father by the power of the Holy Spirit.

24. ON CHRISTIAN FREEDOM

When we speak about freedom we generally make the mistake of asking what we are free *from* rather than what we are free *for*. Protestants are often very proud that the Reformation freed them from the Roman

Catholic Church and its regulations, from its supersti tions and from the authority of the Pope. All this is true, they must be answered, but what king or master do you now acknowledge? It is possible to get free from a false master only by accepting a good one; one is freed from superstition only by true faith, from the false law only by the true law. The man who has simply gotten "free" is without a master and therefore more deeply a slave. For there is no slavery comparable to the slavery of masterlessness. For then a man is slave to his own passions, or to that worst of all tyrants, the Ego, or as the Bible expresses it—to sin. For Master-Ego and sin are exactly the same—the sinful man is the man who recognizes no Lord but himself.

One can get free only by getting free from this Ego-tyrant, sin. This liberation can occur only by the acceptance of God as our Lord. And we accept God as our Lord only by being saved through Christ from our sin. Freedom comes at no lesser price, one cannot underbid Jesus Christ.

"God saw with His eternal grace
My sorrow out of measure:
He thought upon His tenderness—
To save was His good pleasure.

He turned to me a Father's heart;
Not small the cost
To heal my smart:
He gave His best and dearest."

Luther knows what he is saying—the cross of Jesus Christ is the price that had to be paid for our freedom. Not even God could "make it cheaper." Therefore the Apostle Paul says, "Ye are bought with a price; be not ye the servants of men." That is the freedom of a Christian man.

Paul always calls himself a servant of Jesus Christ. And in that servitude is his freedom. We are so created of God that we cannot be free, true men, happy, glad, strong manly men without Him—only through Him. God created us for fellowship with Himself. Fellowship with God is, so to speak, the substance of human life. When we part with God and essay to stand on our own feet, we know our situation to be like that of the son in the parable who said to his father; "Father, give me my inheritance"—then went into the far country and fell into misery. Without God *we* get into the far country and into misery. We waste that "human substance" which consists of fellowship with God and love. The redeeming work of Christ consists in bringing us, the lost, back home to the Father, and thus to liberty.

Only he who has become a "servant of Jesus Christ" is—as Luther says—"a free Lord of all and subject to none, through the faith." He is free from worry—"If God is for us who can be against us?" He is free from human authorities and Lords, from all legalistic service of the letter. Free from the guilt of sin, free from the fear of death—for he has, through Christ, the forgiveness of sins and the promise of eternal life. He no longer needs to observe so and so many hundred laws like the pious Jew or Catholic, but only this one—to remain by God his Father and Lord, bound by no other tie to this Lord and Father except the bond of childlike respect and grateful love. "Love God and do what you want!" was the way the great Augustine phrased it.

Just when one has become free by his reverence and love of God, and by his grateful faith in redemption through Jesus Christ, he is bound to men in a new way. So Luther adds a second statement to his first sentence: "A Christian man is the most dutiful servant of all and subject to every one through love." The slave of sin, slave of his own self is separated from men and wants to dominate them. He must seek his own. He is possessed by selfishness. But he who has been freed by Christ from this worst of all sicknesses and is placed in the love of God, is free *from* himself and free *for* others. The misery and the welfare of other men all at once become important for him. He sympathizes with them, rejoices with them, as though he were one with them. He would be ready to give all things, even his life for the sake of others. That is just the human element which now appears when the inhuman, the sinful has disappeared. He has become a true servant of man—as Jesus was a servant of man.

This freedom, the most glorious thing there is, begins at home. It grows the more we grow into communion with God: it subsides the more we separate ourselves from God. It is the fruit of faith alone. For faith is simply belonging wholly and completely to God. God desires to make us such glad free men through the Gospel.

25. PRAYER

The world often seems like a monstrously sinister machine, blind, insensible, destroying everything that man builds, fosters, loves, hopes. Why should the world concern itself about your wishes, little stupid man? What does your sigh mean in the midst of a universe where suns grow and age in billions of years? Such a thought makes prayer die upon the lips. Is there any sense in praying the roaring avalanche to spare the babe yonder in the path of its downward rush? O fate, blind, awful, senseless fate!

When we look beyond ourselves out into the world, prayer fades away. Man's tragic lot robs one of the courage to pray. Everything appears to be senseless, disorder, chance, confusion. Who then has a mind to pray? The world can at most permit us dimly to perceive a mysterious Power; but to make us trust ourselves to this Power, calling upon it as children do their father: "Help us!" the world is unable. How then can we pray? What gives us the courage, the confidence, the assurance?

As children lost in a woods, are fearful of the sinister darkness—and then, suddenly, hearing a sound from the sombre blackness, a familiar voice, a loving, seeking, helping voice, their mother's voice—so prayer is our reply to the voice from the Word of God in Jesus Christ which suddenly cries out to us in the mysterious, dark universe. It is the Father calling us out of the world's darkness. He calls us, seeks us, wants to bring us to Himself. "Where are you, my child?" Our prayers mean "Here I am, Father. I was afraid until you called. Since you have spoken, I am afraid no longer. Come, I am waiting for you, take me, lead me by the hand through the dark terrifying world."

It is a tremendous moment when a man hears this voice and knows he is safe. God is at hand! The world is not the ultimate, not all. There is a Lord of this world, a ruler over all things; one can call upon Him for He hears. I may say "thou" to Him and it is not merely an echo of my cry that returns to me, but an answer. There is meaning in prayer. Indeed if what has been said is true, not only has prayer meaning but in that meaning is life's most wonderful gift. How a lost explorer, immured upon the floating arctic ice must be encouraged when, thanks to the radio he has with difficulty rescued and set up, he not only sends out the S.O.S. but suddenly hears an answer! New courage and joyful hope mount within him. All can yet come out right. So too of prayer. In the midst of this dark incomprehensible world of fate, of death, it is the invisible contact with Him who is above all, and who calls to us: "Have no fear, I am here, thy Father, thy Creator and Redeemer. I will yet make all things come out right."

Faith lives on prayer, indeed, faith is nothing but prayer. The moment we really believe, we are already praying, and when we cease praying we also cease believing. The philosopher Kant made the statement that prayer obviously has no other effect than that of lifting the spirits of him who prays, and that to assume an effect outside the praying person was unreasonable. No other judgment is possible for the man who does not know the God who speaks to us,—in the sphere of our feelings, perhaps,—but utterly apart from our feelings, in Jesus Christ.

Because they do not know this God and this revelation so many men of our time no longer pray. True prayer is possible only as an answer to God's real revelation. True prayer, that is, prayer in which a man *really* believes he will be heard, is possible only when one believes in the living God. What is meant by the "living God"? The God to Whom you can pray trustfully, because He has previously revealed to you His trustworthiness. That is the living God.

Is it possible, then, for a modern man to pray? There can be no doubt that even the most cultured modern man who has at his disposal all the technical art of our day, needs to pray; indeed, deep in his heart wants to pray. But *can* such a man pray after learning all that he has about the mysterious world-machine, natural laws, and infinity? The modern man, no less than Abraham who looked up and beheld the starry Palestinian heavens 4000 years ago, is a living soul. He is no clod of earth, but an "I." Because of his spirit he is superior to this whole world of matter. My body is a bit of the world, my personality is not. Even the modern man can know that, and many of the clever and learned do know it. Then the question arises, has this personality a Lord, or is it its own master? Is this personality responsible—that is, must it answer Him who calls it, or can it do what it pleases? Responsible man is already addressed by God: "Adam, where art thou?" We are all afraid of this voice, for we know that before it we cannot vindicate ourselves. But the voice which comes thus challenging carries within it that which also cheers: fear not, for I am thy God, thy Father. As surely as even the most modern man is a sinful man who cannot atone for his guilt, so surely the Gospel of the Grace of God is proclaimed to him. Thanks be to God for the many who hear it and henceforth answer God in prayer, with praise, thanks and supplication.

26. THE MEANING OF PRAYER

There is nothing more daring or more humiliating than prayer. It is daring because in prayer I dare to speak with Him whom all the heavens cannot contain. The man who prays trusts that his speaking with God is not in vain, that something happens when he prays that otherwise would not occur. "The fervent prayer of a righteous man availeth much." The brain almost reels when it imagines this possibility, surely it is foolish presumption, or simply a remnant of primitive superstition. Are we to believe that the Lord of the world really considers the petitions brought before him by a mere man? The Bible answers *yes* to all of these questions, and the whole of Biblical revelation creates and nurtures faith in God's hearing of prayer. God is our Father—that means precisely that He hears. He stands in a reciprocal relationship with us, there is communication between us and Him. God awaits our prayer, and because He longs to extend His kingdom not only over men but through men and with men, God accomplishes some things only when they are asked for; God earnestly awaits our prayer. We dare believe that our prayers make possible for us some action of God not otherwise possible. To believe this, and actually to pray in such trust is surely the most daring thing a man can do.

To pray is also most humbling. Every other act, no matter how small or humble, is nevertheless *our* act, we are responsible, it is our work, and we have, for all its insignificance, a certain pride in what we have done. But when we pray we fold our hands in silent gesture that we now do nothing more, we now are at the end of our efforts—that we now leave all things, Father, to Thee! Prayer is a declaration of impotency, it is to say, "I surrender the helm of my life; take it, I can do no more."

Hence prayer is really nothing but faith. So much prayer—so much faith. So little prayer—so little faith. In prayer it appears whether a man is daring enough to believe that God is really our Father. That is trust in God. And in prayer it also appears whether a man is humble enough to surrender all to God and to look for all things from Him. To me it always seems that if we could pray aright great things would have to happen. Christianity is so poverty-stricken because so few really know the meaning of prayer and only he knows who is able to pray. Perhaps none of us yet know rightly. We are still too lacking in trust, and not humble enough in resignation. We do not yet reckon sufficiently on the reality of God. Wherever men today take God with real seriousness miracles happen as they did 2000 years ago. The man who does not believe in such miracles, cannot pray. We fail to take the promises of God seriously enough.

We have to learn how to pray again. It is learned only in quiet and composure. Prayer means first of all the assurance of the presence of God, or as those of old well said "coming before God," "standing before His face." That is not so simple. It requires an effort of the will,—and more than that. "I will arise and go to my Father." That resolution requires the courage to let God tell you the truth, the humiliating knowledge that you can no longer help yourself. Only he really seeks God, for whom all other doors are bolted. God Himself meets us only when we are at the end of our knowledge and power.

Hence prayer is so much harder than work, more exhausting. For a hundred men who are not afraid of the exertion of labor, there are only a few who take upon themselves the strain of prayer. Most flee from it, are afraid of it, for who would not be afraid to be alone with God? To babble little prayers is not to pray.

The Publican who did not dare to lift up his eyes, and who could only sigh "God be merciful to me, a sinner" —prayed. But the Pharisee who used the machinery of prayer so fluently did not pray; he was too full of himself for that.

Prayer, as all worth-while deeds, requires time. He who takes no time for the practice will either fail to learn how to pray, or, if he once knew will soon forget. Only he who takes much time for prayer can then understand what the Apostle means by the word "pray without ceasing." And prayer does not mean saying many words, it means seeking God and letting God seek us. When the Psalmist says that he is still before God, rejoices in God, he indicates the content and the mood of prayer. Prayer proceeds from petition to praise, from praise to thanks; and from praise and thanks onward to enlarged petition. But all real prayer, I think, will begin with the petition of the disciples, "Lord, teach us to pray!"

27. FELLOWSHIP

Many do not know either their own loneliness or the loneliness of others. I do not mean simply that some people are alone. One can be alone and still not be lonely. One can be in a teeming crowd of people and yet be quite lonely. Loneliness is solitude of soul. There are even quite garrulous people who—as it is said—have their hearts on their tongues, and who nevertheless live quite alone. Every person whose life is self-centered has an isolated soul. Such a person is like a castle. There is a gate through which one sallies forth to take booty. There are embrasures through which one shoots poisoned arrows; there are battlements, to be sure, from which one looks down upon those below. But the whole castle is isolated, and over the gate stands "mine" in large letters. The possessor of this castle is called "I." And everything is operated according to the will of this "*I*," and the laws are *my* laws. There is a kind of social life between this feudal lord, the self, and others; there is intercourse, but the spirit of the castle regulates everything. Things must go as *I* want them to, and as they suit *me.* Such a life is isolated, lonesome, even in the midst of the greatest activity. For all people who go in and out are present simply for *my* sake. No one ever enters who is called *thou.*

The castles of mediæval times were sometimes captured by another lord, so—perhaps it may happen to your castle. There is only one who is strong enough to capture it, banish this tyrant named *I,* and revoke *my* law. This one, the only conqueror, conquers not by power or might, blow for blow, by the opposition of his will to the will of the individual. He would accomplish nothing in that way. The Ego has made sufficient provision for assault of this sort. The sole conqueror breaks into the citadel by quite different means. He vanquishes the self through love, by blasting the great gate with forgiveness, by overthrowing the self from the throne by sacrificing, yes even by giving his life for it. This conqueror is called Jesus Christ. And this conquest comes about when the self surrenders like a conquered fort-commander and says, "Enter, thou art now the Lord of my life." This abdication is called faith. Through this event—or rather through Jesus Christ, man is "opened"; the law "for me" is abrogated, and another law introduced—"for you." Solitude ceases the moment the law "for you" takes the place of the other law. Solitude is replaced by fellowship. Fellowship means that the self really dis-closes itself to another, so that "I" and "thou" really come together. Fellowship is the same as love. And this love comes by faith alone, or, what is the same, from Christ alone.

Love thy neighbor as thyself! It is that which Christ

fulfilled, he alone. But by fulfilling it for us, we can now be overcome by him, we too can begin its fulfilment. "Faith working by love." Only in this way can solitude be overcome. Such a new life begins in every man whom Jesus has overcome. Fellowship now displaces loneliness, life is directed toward a *thou* and not toward the self.

It is not, however, only faith that produces fellowship. The reverse is also true. Faith grows out of fellowship. We need others to be able to believe. One cannot be a Christian by himself. All sorts of things can be done alone; but one cannot be a Christian alone. My own weak faith must constantly be awakened, renewed, strengthened, purified by the faith of others. We must come together really to believe. "Where two or three are gathered together in my name, there am I in the midst of them." We must learn that again. Everything today has become a matter of private property and private affairs, even faith. But faith must perish when it is alone. It can thrive only in fellowship.

Our Church is only a remnant of such fellowship. What the Church offers today in the way of fellowship cannot satisfy. It is not enough that the Word of God is proclaimed to you on Sunday, if you are left alone for the remainder of the week. We all need that our faith and prayer should grow strong with the faith of others; and that our own faith and love be increased by and with the faith and love of others. The first Christians remained daily with one another in prayer and breaking of bread. Something of that must come again into our Church. For otherwise all preaching is in vain. If what has been sown on Sunday is not tended in fellowship it is soon lost. The individual is too negligent and weak. "One may fall, but two can stand together." We must open ourselves mutually, otherwise self remains lord, and "for me" the law of life. When we do not share our faith with one another we remain isolated, selfish people. Let us seek the fellowship of faith, according as Christ has opened our hearts.

28. THE CHURCH

"I believe one holy Catholic and Apostolic Church" —so reads the common Christian confession of faith. Almost every word of the sentence is incomprehensible for the present-day man, and even for the average Christian. Luther called the word Church a "blank" and would have preferred the term "the Christian folk." "Church" means for most people the great building with the tower and chimes where every Sunday services of worship are conducted. All of that, to be sure, is used by the Church and reminds us that the matter of greatest significance in the Church is the proclamation of the Gospel. But the misunderstanding is just as great. As if the modest chapel near by were not just as truly a Church! As though there were Church only where there is a clergyman. What is meant in the New Testament by the word we translate "Church"? What is the Church of which the creed speaks?

Church, in Greek is called "ekklesia," which means, —the chosen band. Just as the herald in former times read the royal proclamations in the market-place, and men poured forth from the houses into the square in obedience to his voice and listened to his message; or as the recruiting officer came into a village and with attractive speech won the young men into the army of some great lord,—in similar manner there sounds forth among us God's call to salvation, the "come unto me all ye!" of the world's Saviour. The Company of them that hear and heed this call constitute the "army" of God. The army he has won, "bought with a price," is the Church. Every one who heeds the call of Christ belongs to it, be he Catholic, Quaker, Methodist, or Reformed.

One thing only is decisive: have you really heard, and really heeded the call, or have you made but an exterior gesture of joining this or that? And because this decisive matter can never be seen, judged, or evaluated from the outside, because unlike the military forces of a great king, no one can see or enumerate those who have become part of the "church army" of God, because this hearing and heeding of God's call is a hidden matter, known only to God Himself, we speak also of the invisible Church.

To be sure Christ desires no invisible army. He wants a host of such a kind that even the children of this world, who know nothing of faith nor want to know, will be able to note that there is something mightily at work within these "called-soldiers"; that they obey a mighty Other and no longer their own wills. And Christ now recruits this band through his "recruiting officers" his "heralds." The first heralds were the Apostles and for that reason the Church is called *Apostolic.* The Church rests on them; that is to say, upon the message which they proclaimed, upon the message of Jesus the Son of God, crucified and arisen, the message of the Kingdom and the Reign of God. One belongs to the Church when one is recruited by this message for Christ the King and Lord; and that means belonging to the Kingdom of God, now hidden, until it shall one day be revealed at the time of the end of all things.

This Church is not only "Apostolic," meaning "founded by the Apostles" but it is also *universal.* Formerly it was called "Catholic," but every man understands by that the Roman Catholic Church, which is something quite different. Universal means spread over the whole world. *One* army—whether in Switzerland or in America or in Japan, wherever men "call upon the name of the Lord Jesus" at all times and in all places. Universal, too, in the sense that it cuts across all state churches, confessions, and sects. Christ does not have all his people in one body; they are not only scattered about through all lands, but are among all church organizations. The Roman Catholics rightly lament this latter fact. There should be but one Church. How much more driving power it would have, how much greater its impact on the world! And conversely: how the name of Jesus is blasphemed because there are so many churches, sects, and confessions! Why is it so? Because people did not remain in the truth, that is to say, the truth the Apostles proclaimed. And also because pride, contentiousness, and pomposity supposed something additional was necessary, something beyond the hearing and the heeding of God's call. Sects have been formed for all sorts of insignificant reasons; for the most part, to be sure, because some established "church" had gone spiritually to sleep or had languished. There should be only one Church, but this unity can come only from a powerful renewal of faith, a new Reformation created out of the depths of the Gospel.

The most important and difficult word is the *Holy* Church. Holy doesn't mean what one usually understands it to signify, but means "belonging to God." That is definitive not only for the Church, but for eternal life also. He who does not belong to God and who has not really been enlisted, cannot be saved and must be lost. A man belongs to God and becomes holy by accepting the divine promise of forgiveness in repentance and faith. When that occurs another person is received into the Church, a new member grows upon the body "whose head is Christ." How does one get into the Church? Solely and simply by a hearty trust in and obedience to the Word of God. To establish "obedience to the faith among all nations" was the purpose of Paul in setting forth, and it was in this way that he enlisted the Church, the Army of God. Obedience to the faith is the touchstone of true Church membership.

29. THE SACRAMENTS

Even most good Christians do not know what to make of the Sacraments: Baptism and the Lord's Supper. They are venerable customs which have always been performed by the Church, in which one takes part out of respect, or because they are here and are observed —or perhaps simply out of habit, or "because it makes things better." In the cities, the neglect of the Lord's Supper is quite general. Often no more than a fourth of the many who throng the church on high festivals remain for the Lord's Supper. Are the Sacraments dying branches on the tree of the Church—like so much that once was customary, but is now sacrificed to the times?

The Lord surely knew what he was doing when, on that last night, he said to his Disciples, "This do in remembrance of me." Without the Sacraments the Church would long ago have disappeared, and with the passing of the Church would have gone also Christian faith and the Bible. The Sacraments are the divinely given flying buttresses which save the Church from collapse. In how many of the Churches of today do we not find the Sacraments almost the sole biblical footing —the only biblical element that has been able to withstand the caprices of the gifted minister who lives by his own wisdom rather than from the Scriptures. Even the most audacious minister has not dared to lay hands on the Sacraments. And they are what they are! One may so interpret the words of Scripture that the words speak the opposite of their intent; but the Sacraments, thank God, speak a language independent of the language of the Pastor. They are a part of the message of the Church least affected by theological or other tendencies; and that is their especial blessing.

Yes, the Sacraments have a message for us. God wants to speak to us in them. For once, however, He addresses us through the eye, instead of through the ear as in preaching, through an action instead of through speech. Thus we cannot have the excuse that since the concrete appeals to us more than the abstract we cannot understand the message of the Church.

The Sacraments are God's message for the eye, for the whole body. One eats and drinks, the whole man partakes of the Sacrament. It is, however, not eating and drinking alone, but surely solely and simply permitting God to say what He wants to impart to us, which is just nothing but the Gospel, laid hold upon at its heart in the message of the Cross. To receive and embrace God's Word in the Sacrament, this alone matters. God *acts* upon us in the Lord's Supper. As the Pastor distributes the bread and wine to you, God distributes His grace. He is present in this action—whether the Pastor is a believer or not—God is present therein in such a way as to be able to touch your heart, humbling and exalting you, bringing you to repentance and faith.

Why is it necessary to have this special way of speaking God's Word, if it still says nothing more than the sermon? Because in the Sacrament the Word seeks us in a different mode, and through a different channel, not with many words, but in an intelligible *act.* Above all, the consideration is important that you can have the spoken Word of God at home, not only in the Bible, since even the sermon is now being "delivered to your own home" as is everything else, by radio. This convenience may have many advantages. But one inherent evil develops almost of necessity; people do not come *together* to hear God's Word and to thank God for it in prayer and song. One becomes a private Christian, one does not know any more the meaning of Church, or the fellowship of faith. The fellowship of faith is, however, an integral part of faith. It is possible to enjoy a work of art, a concert or a lecture, and be edified by it without the presence of any other person. Enjoyment and edification in these spheres do not require the presence of others. One cannot have faith alone. Indeed the aim of the Word of God is to conquer this solitude by leading us out of our isolation into fellowship with one another. God's Word and fellowship are inseparable. Therefore our Lord instituted the Sacraments that we might not make a private concern of His Word, but come together *actually,* not simply "in spirit."

The Sacraments bind us to the Church. They are acts requiring the presence of several; acts in which it becomes clear that one receives God's salvation, yes, truly receives it through the mediation of a man. God wants to give us the highest gifts through men, that we in coming to Him, might also come to men. He wants to draw us out of our isolation and self-satisfaction. He wants to lead us to others in such a way that we perceive our need of them. Christians are men who have felt their need of others. So often it is just the "good" and "able" people who fail to see this. "I can get along by myself." It is just that which is sin, pride, and lovelessness. God did not create us to be able to get along by ourselves, but that we "should bear one another's burdens." The Sacraments are the buttresses which keep the Church from falling asunder because they do not permit a man to receive the salvation of God alone. Only in the congregation, only in confessing "I need the other man" shall you receive God's salvation. Otherwise you remain self-contained—and unsaved.

30. BAPTISM

Few of the readers of this book are not baptized, but there are not very many who know what it means to be baptized. "Well, a person has to have a name," and that is what one gets in baptism! Aren't warships "christened" when they get their names? No. You received a name when a county official entered you in the Birth Register; no baptism was necessary for such a purpose.

In former times slaves were branded on the back with their master's name. In your baptism God laid hold upon you, called you by your name and stamped you as ever after—His own. Through the word and act of man in your baptism, the brand, "property of God" was stamped upon you. The words "God's own" were spoken over you by the Church, the Church of Jesus Christ; God has laid claim upon you through the act of the Church.

Do we not belong to God without Baptism, by virtue of being His creatures? To be sure. We should not know this if God had not said so in His Word; without God's Word we know neither Him nor ourselves. Without God's Word we do not know we are His property and all that this ownership means for our lives. In His Son, our Lord Jesus Christ, God has shown us *what* it means to be His property and *how* He is disposed toward us. God does not make us His property in Jesus Christ to show that He can do with us what He wills, as the slaveholder stamps His name upon His slaves. He can to be sure, do with us what He wills; He is the Creator and we are His creatures. He does not want us to have to be afraid of Him as slaves before their master, but rather to love Him as the one who first loved us. "God so loved the world that He gave his only begotten Son that whosoever believeth in Him should not perish but have everlasting life." *That* is the Gospel, in *this* way God claims us, in *this* way He means to proclaim to us by the Church the words, "Thou art mine."

Baptism is the prevenient love of God antecedent to any human effort. What did we know when our sponsors held us, crying infants, up to the Pastor for Baptism! He "received us in love before we ever thought of Him." He gave us a name that is written in no Civil Register—child of God! He has been before-hand with His gift; He loved us even before we were as yet conscious of our identity.

Are we then children of God by virtue of Baptism? Is it so simple and so cheap? Yes—if you believe. "Whosoever believeth in Him. . . ." Indeed faith is not so simple and cheap. Baptism wants to point out just that. Baptize comes from "baptizo" to dip. Children formerly were not simply sprinkled with water, but immersed, and so, too, were the first Christian adults baptized. Why was this done? As a sign that we must die really to belong to God. We are baptized into the *death* of our Lord. We must share in his death if we desire to share in his life. We are by nature men who do not at all desire to belong to God, but to themselves. The "Lord" of our life says first, I am the Lord *my* God! This self-willed, self-seeking, self-glorifying *I* must be drowned. And that is not so "cheap and easy." It costs much. It cost the Lord Jesus his life. "To believe" that we belong to God, means no less than to be crucified with Jesus Christ, knowing that he had to die for us, trusting that he really died for us—really for you—and therewith setting aside all that separates us from God. "The old Adam in us should, by daily sorrow and repentance be drowned and die," says Luther. Every day we must be immersed anew in the divine forgiveness, and repent, put off what separates us from God. Baptism itself happens just once. But we must believe constantly anew, for only through faith does Baptism save us. "That whosoever believeth in Him. . . ." Hence we are not baptized merely in the name of the Father and of the Son, but also of the Holy Ghost. "Now if any man have not the Spirit of Christ, he is none of His."

31. THE LORD'S SUPPER

Concerning nothing in the Christian Church has there been more dispute than over the Lord's Supper, which was surely intended solely as a means of fellowship. Concerning few things have so abstruse theological dogmas been formulated as there have been concerning the Lord's Supper, which was surely intended solely as a divine help in understanding the message of reconciliation, a perceptual picture of the heart of the Gospel, the superb gift with which God longs to draw us to Himself.

The Lord's Supper—and this must be said first of all—is not magic but, so to speak, an "illustrated word of God," given in order that we might not merely hear the message of divine grace, but also see it and perceive it the more clearly. This is all that happens; but of course this "all" is the inexhaustible miracle of divine reconciliation.

Bread and wine are distributed in the Lord's Supper. We are to eat and drink, which means that we are to receive that by which we live. But this bread and this wine are signs, symbols. The spiritual bread of life and the spiritual drink of life is—Christ himself. "I am the Bread of Life. He that believeth on me shall never thirst." This "he that believeth" in the utterance of Jesus is a great mystery; it is likewise the great mystery of the Lord's act in giving us the Sacrament of his Supper. This holy act is a means which God employs to give us His Word, Jesus Christ; to strengthen and nourish that faith with which alone we receive Christ. *God* then, not simply the pastor and the deacons, does something in the Lord's Supper. Not simply bread and wine but Christ himself is present in the Sacrament. Indeed, Christ the Bread of Life, and not simply natural bread, is to be eaten. It is a miracle that God should speak His Word to us, and that we should receive and eat it in faith. As surely as simple natural bread is eaten, and this natural bread is and remains bread, so surely something else is also eaten—the Word of God, Christ, the Bread of Life. Both really eaten, the one physically, the other spiritually. The soul is just as real as the body and must, with equal reality, be nourished. But as the soul is invisible, it must be nourished with invisible bread. Christ is the Bread of the soul, just as wheat bread is the nourishment of the body.

It is no mere chance that we use bread and wine in the Sacrament. Jesus instituted the Lord's Supper the night before his crucifixion. He broke the bread as a symbol for his body which was to be broken on the following morning. So, too, the wine to signify his blood. The Lord's Supper "proclaims" the "Lord's death." It is a narrative, but more than that, for it transmits at the same time the significance of this death.

When a man dies, the significance of his death for him and for his loved ones is that he is no longer present. Jesus' death is, however, no such human death. The death of Jesus is something that God does to help the whole world. The death of Jesus is the atoning act of God. It is this death which the Lord's Supper proclaims, this perishing whereby *we* receive eternal life. In the Lord's Supper God would say to us that this death is your life, if you in faith partake of him. By faith you are united with the crucified and risen Christ; by faith you, the sinner, come to the Cross and this eternal life comes to you. By faith you receive what is Christ's and he takes upon himself what is yours. This inconceivable exchange—is the grace of God in Jesus Christ.

You receive this grace through God's Word, be it through the word the preacher proclaims from the pulpit, or by what the Lord's Supper says to you of God's grace. It wants to tell you *that!* So to tell it that you can also see it, better understand it, and more certainly believe it.

One thing more. It is just by this act of the Lord's Supper that we are told clearly that we can have God's salvation only in fellowship; not each one for himself alone. The Lord's Supper is an act of fellowship. We are not only to be united with Christ, but also with our fellow men. "One body whose head is Christ." When there is one body, each member thinks and suffers for the other. Whoever goes away from the Lord's Supper without the love of the brethren being awakened in him, has received nothing; he was present in vain, for it is by our love to the brethren that we prove we have fellowship with Christ.

32. THE FUTURE

The Christian faith is distinguished from all other faiths in that it knows that God is coming. That God shall come to His people is the great theme of the Old Testament; and the first word of the New Testament hails Him, "Repent for the Kingdom of Heaven is at hand." The whole long record closes with the beautiful prayer, "Even so, Come, Lord Jesus!" The proclamation of the coming reign of God is the Gospel, and the assurance of future salvation and eternal completion is the Christian faith.

The great human sorrow is hopelessness, and hopelessness reigns wherever men do not know that God is coming, for hopelessness muses, the world cannot be helped and *I* cannot be helped. To be sure people do hope, but they hope only for the "improvement" which comes with development. One hopes in the "healthy kernel" the "good forces operative in us" and the like. Such hope is no real hope. If we must rely solely upon our own potencies, on the powers latent in the world, we are lost. Development of our own strength or release of the energies of the universe cannot redeem us from the corruption that death and sin signify. If we are to rely solely upon ourselves, what is in us and in the world, then everything still ends in one great bankruptcy.

The Bible tells us we are not thrown upon our own resources. The world is not "closed" but open to God. You are not isolated, but open in God's direction; or rather, God relieves your isolation. God breaks into the world. He breaks open the dungeon to release the languishing prisoners and bring them to the light of day. He comes to His corrupt creation to restore its original goodness and to perfect it. God comes to *you* to save *you!* When we hear that proclamation two questions arise, How does this happen, and how does one know it is so? Both questions have *one* answer, Jesus Christ. Because we know Jesus Christ, we know what is meant by the coming of God, the new redemption. And because we know Jesus Christ we know that this redemption is really true. We are not speaking of theories or of heartening thoughts, but of something that has occurred. "The life was manifested and we have seen it, and bear witness, and shew unto you that eternal life, which was with the Father, and was manifested unto us."

God *has* already come. "The Word *became* flesh and we *beheld* His glory." Jesus Christ has become real history, and in him the great new thing has come, a thing that the world does not have, and that you do not possess—life from God, love, the love of God that forgives us our sin and heals our diseases.

With Jesus came the Kingdom of God. Something new is now in the world that was not previously here, fellowship with God by faith, the peace of God that passes all understanding, life in communion with God and man, a life in the Holy Spirit. There is now a Church of Christ in which he himself is the head and men are the members, head and members united with one another, a "communion of saints"—men not holy in themselves and by themselves, but made holy by fellowship with him. The Kingdom of God actually exists wherever living faith and living love grows out of communion with God.

This new life in God is something infinitely great and precious, this new joy, certainly of God, this new power, new will, new fellowship with one another. "If any man be in Christ, he is a new creature, old things are passed away; behold all things are become new."

This new life does not obliterate, but must abide in the old life. Hence it is a *hidden* new life, just as the glory of God and the reign of God in Jesus Christ were concealed under the humiliation of a Cross and the form of a servant. The new is in process of becoming, it struggles out of the old. As a clear strong shaft of light is broken and diffused in passing through a dark glass, so the new Christ-life, itself so clear and strong, must yet shine through "the old Adam." "It doth not yet appear what we shall be." We all are, and indeed remain sinners, those who have fellowship with God. We sigh under the burden of our own imperfection, we are shamed again and again by the corruption the old Adam ever holds between us and the new life. We long for perfection, but we know that we must die, and know also that death is simply the judgment upon the old Adam, the old nature we ever carry about with us. The

Kingdom of God has not yet come in its fulness. We therefore look into the future, God's future. What we already have is just the pledge of what is to come. But what will come is not "something" but *He Himself*. Without the prospect of the future there remains only illusion or despair. Illusions that delude us about the frailty of our present possessions, despair that shuts out the hope for the future. Faith is not merely an uncertain longing, an indefinite expectation, but the soul's open window to the future, the glad assurance of that which is promised us in Christ. Such is the true Christian nature which is born of God; it "waits upon God."

33. AFTERWARD?

What is coming? We are not prophets. Even for our own little lives we cannot, with any degree of certainty, prognosticate one day ahead. It is probable that so and so will occur tomorrow, but all may turn out quite differently. On one matter only are we real prophets, we can predict with utter certainty that death is coming. And yet, in spite of our certain knowledge that we must die, the thought plays a very small rôle in our life. We avoid this thought, it is painful, indeed, fearful to us.

For death means all is over; if there is nothing more, then every column in this life adds up to the same result —zero. Death means that everything we create, the purposes for which we struggle, the ends after which we strive, for which we make sacrifices—all are at last nothing. Death finally destroys all; all that is, is fit for destruction. Do not say that all high purposes and noble ends will continue to live in those who follow. Say rather that all will ultimately die with those dying men who follow us. All paths lead into—the grave. That is the fearful geography of this life. It is no wonder that we avoid this thought.

To evade is not finally to escape, for this thought is swifter and stronger than our evasion. The fear of death accompanies us secretly in everything we do or leave undone, everything we think or say. It is the quiet undertone that penetrates all life. What Christ says is true of every one—the courageous and the unconcerned, the cowardly and the careful, "In the world ye shall have tribulation." To each one it comes in a different form. We live like business men, who foresee certain bankruptcy but do not dare think of it, do not any longer balance books, make no attempt to save themselves. Fate must ultimately overtake us; so let us make shift of our days well as we can! Afterward comes the end!

Is death really the end? Is life then really senseless? Death, nothingness, is the most senseless thing we can imagine. And this is indeed the final result. But we know that in a religious, assuredly in a Christian book, we must expect to read a denial of the total destructive power of death, and that there is indeed an eternal life. But do we really believe it? And is it so sure? Can one know something certain about the matter? Death is that "undiscovered country from whose bourne no traveller returns." So, then, what we have are not certainties but only beautiful comforting auto-suggestions that may be true, that may be quite false. Isn't this the way we naturally think? That we do so think is because we doubt. And many have the idea that doubt belongs to life and cannot be helped, that it belongs even to the Christian life.

But the truth is that so long as we are in bondage to this doubt we are not yet Christians. For to doubt eternal life is to dismiss the promises of God, to be disobedient to the Word of God, to put our trust in our own understanding and senses. God's Word is not sufficient guarantee, we want something more certain. But this desire for something more certain than God's Word *is* doubt, crass, naked doubt; crass, naked paganism; crass, naked Godlessness.

The Word of God is the message of eternal life. Jesus Christ came to show us eternal life and to bestow it upon us. "I am the resurrection and the Life. He that believeth in me, though he were dead, yet shall he live: and whosoever liveth and believeth in me shall never die." That is Christ's message. Whosoever is not sure of this in his faith should not think that he is a Christian.

Can one "believe" such a thing? One can, of course, say the words, but the mere words give no help. Doubt continues to live under the same roof with this "faith"; this "faith" has no power, for it does not overcome our terror of death. Hence the Lord says, "He that believeth in me, *hath* eternal life." So believing in Christ, then, is not merely "believing" but life itself! Eternal life! Eternal life begins where fellowship with Christ begins, and when this begins, doubt disappears. Because Christ comes into a man's life, doubt must disappear. Christ and doubt cannot exist together. Christ alone can overcome doubt, Christ alone can really free us from the fear of death. And by doing that he makes us joyful men. "In the world ye shall have tribulation, but be of good cheer, for I have overcome the world." It is as though he said to you, "If you are alone you are afraid. But I have overcome your fear by standing beside you." Upon some mountain peaks there is only one solitary path—and he who will not climb through this narrow place cannot reach the summit and must fall to his death. So, too, there is only one way to eternal life—Christ. He who passes him by misses the goal and falls into the abyss. But he who finds this way is saved, from doubt, from tribulation and from death itself.

34. THE LAST JUDGMENT

"The history of the world is the judgment of the world," says Schiller. The Bible not only does not contest this statement, but repeatedly confirms it. That the judgment of God prevails in history, as well as in the life of the individual, is the meaning of the stories of the Flood and the tower of Babel, in which God judges in catastrophe the blasphemous deeds of men. They relate how God steps into history with His storms and upheavals to shatter those moments of human madness in which self-drunken men raise their towers to heaven. The Bible teaches us to observe how "he that soweth to the flesh shall of the flesh reap corruption." It shows us how "righteousness exalteth a nation, but sin is a reproach to any people," and that this is true of great and small, of the life of the Nations as of individuals. These are indeed judgments, but they are not "The Judgment." These judgments have been or are being completed in history, they are but preludes to "The Judgment," which has not yet come. These judgments give us a preview, as it were of the Last Judgment.

"We must all appear before the Judgment seat of Christ; that every one may receive the things done in his body, according to that he hath done, whether it be good or bad." "God will render to every man according to his deeds: to them who by patient continuance in well-doing seek for glory and honor and immortality, eternal life: but unto them that are contentious, and do not obey the truth, but obey unrighteousness, indignation and wrath." It is no Jewish moralist who tells us *that,* but the Apostle through whom God has most powerfully proclaimed the message of His forgiving love.

One scarcely hears a sermon any more about The Judgment. Perhaps in former times there was too much and too rash preaching on this subject, motivated by a desire to drive men into the Kingdom of Heaven by fear. No one enters into the Kingdom of Heaven by fear, and the man who tries to do God's will out of fear simply does not do God's will. He alone can do God's will who loves God with all his heart, and trusts Him and relies wholly upon His mercy, but just because we must constantly take refuge in God's mercy, and not go our independent way, we need the message of the Judgment. We need it, just because we learn from it to "bring forth fruits meet for repentance." Every man, believer or unbeliever ought to know that at last comes the Judgment when the Shepherd of Nations will separate the sheep from the goats. "Then shall the King say unto them on His right hand, Come, ye blessed of my Father, inherit the Kingdom prepared for you from the foundation of the world." "Then shall He say also unto them on the left hand, Depart from me, ye cursed, into everlasting fire, prepared for the devil and his angels." These words are not an opinion, they are the Lord's words (Matt. 25). So God speaks to each one of us, and whether or not we want to hear Him is not a matter of choice or speculation.

The message of the Judgment informs us that God is to be taken seriously, that God will not be mocked. It tells us that God is not only the loving Father, but also the righteous Lord, who desires that His commandments find obedience.

"We must all," says Paul, "appear before the Judgment seat of Christ and must testify." "Who then can be saved?" the troubled disciples asked their Lord. "With men it is impossible, but with God all things are possible," he gave answer.

Therefore the message of the Cross of Christ is given us, that it might show us the mercy of God with whom all things are possible. This message, however, does not mean, as it has often been interpreted, that the Judgment no longer means anything to him who believes in Christ, but rather that he alone survives the Judgment who has become a new man through faith in Christ, who has "passed from death to life" and hence belongs among those who "by patient continuance in well-doing seek for eternal life." God alone knows which are the good trees, that bear good fruit. We men can deceive ourselves. We know this much for certain, however, that no one is a "good tree" that rests upon his own righteousness.

We understand what the Bible tells us about forgiveness only when we take seriously what it says about the Judgment. Only then do we really know what the

Scriptures mean by "repent and be baptized in the name of the Lord Jesus," for it is this name alone that sustains us on that day. But the Lord Jesus can help us then only when he knows us to be his own, and does not have to say, "I know ye not." "For not every one that saith unto me, Lord, Lord, will enter the Kingdom of Heaven, but he that doeth the will of my Father which is in heaven." This word, too, we must "let remain." It belongs to the word of Judgment, not to make us afraid, but to drive us to repentance, that we might really become those who "are His" by faith, hope, and love.

35. ON LIFE ETERNAL

Of ourselves we know only that all things die! What our eyes see and experience daily is that there is nothing perfect. When we look about on this great universe, we shudder. In the midst of infinite space, with its millions of suns that arise and grow old in millions upon millions of years, what does this little earth-history mean? In the midst of the history of man, where races stream forth as from an inexhaustible spring into visible life and then disappear again after a few short centuries of stardom—what is the meaning of your insignificant life with its seventy, or "by reason of strength" eighty years? Is there any meaning to it at all? No, says the universe to us. Yes, says the Word of God, the Creator of all these suns and races is thy Creator. The tremendous starry world that frightens you is not the real world. This racial life with its waxing and waning is not real life, this is all only on the surface. Beyond it is another life, that longs to break forth. It has broken forth once in Jesus Christ, the Risen Lord, and it will break forth for us all in the Resurrection. This other life is *Eternal* life. Eternal life is not an unending continuance of this life—that would perhaps be Hell—but Eternal life is a quite different life, divine, not mundane, perfect, not earthly, true life, not corrupt half-life.

We cannot form a conception of eternal life. What we imagine is ever simply of the earth, temporal, worldly. Nor could we know anything about our eternal life if it had not appeared in Jesus Christ. In him we realize that we were created for the eternal life. If we ask what is this eternal life? What sense is there in thinking about it if we can have no conception of it? the answer is, "It is life *with* God, *in* God, *from* God; life in perfect fellowship." Therefore it is a life in love, it is love itself. It is a life without the nature of death and of sin, hence without sorrow, pain, anxiety, care, misery. To know this suffices to make one rejoice in eternal life.

If there were no eternal life, this life of time would be without meaning, goal, or purpose, without significance, without seriousness and without joy. It would be nothing, for what ends in nothing, is itself nothing. That our life does not end in nothing, but that eternal life awaits us is the glad message of Jesus Christ. He came to give us this promise as a light in this dark world. A Christian is a man who has become certain of eternal life through Jesus Christ.

What is the meaning of life? There are many answers to this question. It means power, possessions, honor, progress, culture, etc. That is not the true answer. If that is all life means then our answer is no answer at all, because surely all these things end in nothing. The true answer is that the meaning of this life is *eternal* life. Such is its seriousness. The stakes are high, the loss or gain of eternal life. The dice are cast for a great prize—how have your dice fallen? Do you win eternal life, or do you lose it? How does one win eternal life? "Master, what must I do to inherit eternal life?" That question was answered, "Keep the commandments!" "What must I do to be saved?" That question was answered, "Believe on the Lord Jesus Christ!" Which answer is correct? Both mean the same thing—become a child of God! How a man can become a child of God has been the theme of this whole book. A child of God is, as the Scripture says, an heir of eternal life.

Death ends all life on this earth. We shall all die some day. Tomorrow? Next year? It makes no difference. Some day! Even the whole race will one day die. Without faith that means all is over. But faith says: the end is eternal life.

Is it certain that faith is right? Can one know that so certainly? In the last analysis is it not a supposition? When this question arises—and why should it not arise?—we find out whether we can really believe. Faith is the assurance that God has truly revealed His will to us in Jesus Christ, and this will is eternal life. *How* he will realize his will we do not know, the "how" is unimportant for us. Our business is to live in this faith, to be joyful, and to live even now in this love which is the inner meaning of eternal life. Eternal life begins by faith in Christ, and when it has begun death can have no more dominion over us.